Robert J. Kravitz

A Collector's Guide to Postage & Fractional Currency

The Pocket Change of the Union

Second Edition

I0806778

Coin & Currency Institute
82 Blair Park Road #399, Williston, Vermont 05495
(802) 878-0822 • Fax (802) 536-4787 • E-mail: info@PaperMoneyoftheUS.com

A Collector's Guide to Postage & Fractional Currency

THE POCKET CHANGE OF THE UNION

ISBN-13: 978-087184-204-6 ISBN-10: 087184-204-1

OTHER BOOKS PUBLISHED BY THE COIN & CURRENCY INSTITUTE

PAPER MONEY OF THE UNITED STATES

GOLD COINS OF THE WORLD

COINS OF THE BRITISH WORLD

APPRAISING AND SELLING YOUR COINS

SO-CALLED DOLLARS

AMERICA'S FOREIGN COINS

INVESTOR'S GUIDE TO UNITED STATES COINS

MODERN WORLD COINS

CURRENT COINS OF THE WORLD

COINAGE & CONFLICT

THE EARLY DATED COINS OF EUROPE: 1234–1500

THE COMPLETE CATALOG OF UNITED STATES LARGE SIZE STAR NOTES 1910–1929

A publication of

Coin & Currency Institute

Printed in the United States of America

SECOND EDITION

CREDITS

This book could not have been completed without the pioneering efforts of several authors. A full bibliography appears in the rear matter, but several contributors stand out as follows:

Permission Granted for the use of the term "Fr." for Friedberg Numbers published in *Paper Money of the United States*, Coin and Currency Institute.

Thanks also to Milton R. Friedberg for permission to use his numbering system denoted, "Milt#" as used in his reference book, *The Encyclopedia of United States Fractional & Postal Currency.*

I am also indebted to Jerry Fochtman for compiling his CD of color pictures of fractional notes.

ACKNOWLEDGMENTS

I would like to thank the many people who have encouraged me in this endeavor over the years.

Special Thanks to Eric P. Newman for the use of his amazing library in the late 1960s when I was just starting with Fractionals. I learned a lot and am still learning everyday because of that experience.

Marlin Kravtiz, Tom Kolbrener and Barry Faintich for their early encouragement.

Ray Ellenbougen for his guidance and wisdom and of course Milton Friedberg for his Herculean work on Fractionals and for being the best at helping the world identify every singlenote.

Larry Brasler for all his help with wide-margin proofs.Mike Marchioni for his unparalleled knowledge of the true rarities and high grade notes.

Hank Harrison and Catriona Watson at Arkives Publishing, for making it possible.

Cherie Schoeps for translating my early scribblings into readable information.

Thanks also to Don Kagin, Judy Kagin Benny Bolin, Louis DeSantis, Howard, Cohen, Jerry Fochtman, Rick Melamed, Thomas F.C. O'Mara, Art Paradis, T.C. Clark, Martin Gengerke, Jerry Hoffman, The "Musk", Phil Stangler, and John and Nancy Wilson.

CONTENTS

FOREWARD

In many instances, coin and currency dealers make a transition from collector/hobbyist to dealer, Rob Kravitz was no exception. Rob began collecting fractional currency in the mid 1960s, managed a coin shop in St. Louis in the 1970s, worked at his father's auto parts store and, for a brief period in his life, was a professional foosball (table soccer) player. When, in 1976, he decided to become a professional currency and coin dealer, his fractional currency collection comprised a large portion of his inventory.

I first met Rob at the 1977 International Paper Money Show in Memphis, Tennessee. As I recall, at 9:00 am, people were lined up twenty deep at the Rivermont Holiday Inn. As I made my way through the bourse in search of currency dealers I recognized, I viewed the stock of Ted Kemm, Don DeVore, Richard Picker, Lou Michaels and Len Glazer. Finally, I came to a table with an extensive array of high quality fractional currency, but a dealer whom I did not recognize - Robert Kravitz. After spending about a half hour viewing Rob's stock, I chose a note that was missing from my regular issue collection,. I asked Rob if the listed price was what he wanted for the note, and he kindly responded that he could discount the note by ten percent. I happily accepted his offer and quickly became the new owner of the finest known, Fr. 1286, inverted "S".

Through the years, Rob has been one of the mainstays among fractional currency dealers. Even during the doldrums of the fractional currency market (1983-1994), Rob was still actively buying and selling fractionals. His reference library and knowledge level has grown significantly since the early days of the 1970s. His grading skills are among the best of the paper money dealers. Today, he is arguably the premier dealer in high-quality fractional currency in the United States (my apologies to Tom Denly, Len Glazer, Jim Polis and friends.)

From then on I remained in the business of selling Fractional Currency even when I moved to the West Coast and started selling auto parts again.

It was an honor to be on the floor at the first Paper Money Show in Memphis, June, 1977, but I was still a little wet behind the ears. I sold Mike Marchioni a nice note in great shape for $40.00. Twenty years later, Mike told me that note was a rare inverted "S"-type. I quickly looked it up and discovered that the note was worth $2,800.00 on today's market. That's when I realized a modern and updated price guide needed to be published. We live and learn. I hope you can learn from my mistakes.

As you move thought the book I hope you will learn the professional terms and the catalog references codes that will help you identify the notes you have in your collection. I also hope you can use my book to evaluate the condition and potential value of your notes.

Thanks for your interest.

RJK

PREFACE

Most people, even highly educated people, are surprised when they discover that paper money in small denominations was a direct result of the Civil War. In fact, postage stamps were once used as currency but the stamps were too small and difficult to use, so, during the Civil War, a new kind of paper money called "Postage Currency" was issued by the Union Government to take the place of the increasingly valuable copper, silver and gold coins that had been popular in America since Colonial times. The metallic coinage,

especially silver and gold, became so valuable that certain avaricious citizens, bankers and opportunists, began to hoard them. These private caches became so large that coinage, as known in the mid-19th century, was almost wiped out.

As the public became more insecure and the economy was again impacted by the disappearance of metal coinage. The average family held back coins and started stashing them in the barn or in the sock drawer, not out of greed, but as a hedge against future collapse. Many folks in the North thought the South might win. The issuance of paper money helped save the economy of the North by making it possible to do every day business without metal coins. Something similar happened in the South and today all of the monetary examples are fervently collected. Needless to say, most of the substitute or surrogate monies, be they coins, wooden nickels, stamps, or bits of old coffee cans, are valuable and continued to increase in value.

Most experts agree that the first postage currency in the North was issued by an army paymaster in Philadelphia, Pennsylvania. If you were to sort the contents of a northern soldiers pockets in late August, 1862, you might be surprised to find no coins, a wallet containing a family picture perhaps, but you would also surely find an odd assortment of colored bits of paper with numbers and writing printed on them. These strange objects, fractional currency, allowed the soldiers to buy the necessities of life, and provided for their families, but everyday civilians also used the fractionals to buy staples and goods. John S. Knox, in his history of Greenbacks, said: "The little notes were stuffed into the trouser pocket of the soldier, with his pen knife, cartridges, a plug of tobacco, and other handy articles."

In this way fractional currency became an important part of the Civil War. These colorful notes saw duty at all the major battlefields of the war, including Gettysburg, Bull Run, and Shiloh, and this kind of money was soon adopted by the public.

We Need a New Book!

For the past thirty years, and especially since the turn of the Mil lennium, customers and friends have been urging me to put out my own book on Fractionals. Today's prices on fractional and postage currency are set by men and women who have been in the field for years, dealers who use well established numismatic criteria to evaluate the examples and they traditionally use rarity and condition as two major criteria.

The condition of a note is not always obvious, some are borderline, with very subtle differences between a clean note and a "not so clean" note. They can be graded by experts and the rarity established by historical research. This is done by going back to record books and deciphering just how many were issued, how many have shown up in dealer's inventory and the interest in the collecting community for the note. When one compares rarity, condition and price, it becomes quite clear that almost perfect notes are hard very to find. These are called GEM quality notes and the next step below GEM is CHCU for "Choice Uncirculated." We will discuss the entire grading system later, but for now let's just understand that notes in this condition are a great value and may increase in value every year, faster than gold in an inflationary market. The word is now out thanks to eBay and other outlets. Many new collectors are on the prowl for bargains.

How can I say this for sure? Well for one thing the subscription rate to Banknote Reporter is up significantly and the membership is also up in the Fractional Currency Collector's Board which is the club for Fractional Currency collectors. (See List)

The rise in value of Fractionals has recently been driven, by several phenomena. First, most of the older collections have been broken up or sold intact at auctions and estate sales over the past decade. The old guard is passing on the lamp, as it were. Secondly, most serious new collectors are fairly young and will not be selling for many years to come. This has a tendency to slow down the market for the more pristine items, especially the rarities. It is thus, increasingly difficult to obtain high grade or rare fractionals. Fewer

Gems and quality rare notes are coming up for sale and when they do, their value is market driven. Not only is there a great increase in the number of fractional note collectors, there has also been a large increase in the number of dealers stocking fractionals. But who can afford to buy these things? Well, that surprises me too. The Gem quality items may be hard to find, but great examples of many notes still exist at reasonable prices.

I'm writing this book in hopes of clarifying the controversies surrounding these notes and this field of collecting, but I repeat, obtaining a specific fractional note in Gem or CU condition has become quit a challenge, even for well-established collectors with contacts far and wide.

Later on you will see the catalog designations and current prices laid out in tabular form, but for now let me simply quote a few examples of rarity. In the most prominent case, the 50¢, fifth issue Crawford note (catalog # Fr. 1381) is common, but not usually found in a pristine version. A couple of years ago, it took me six months to find a true Gem "Crawford" to complete a twenty-three piece set. Also the 50¢, fiber paper, autographed signature, red back, Justice note (catalog # Fr. 1357) is very scarce, they come up for sale maybe once per year. There are now only twenty three uncirculated notes of this number known, and only one in GEM. So, if you want to put a GEM, forty-three piece set together, you'll have to settle for a "filler" of a lesser quality or come up with a magic wand and a fistful of modern dollars. Another example is the 25¢, third issue, (catalog # Fr. 1296), of which there are only twelve notes known. I know where ten of them are, and these collectors have no plans to sell any of them in the near future. According to treasury records, this leaves only two notes that may, someday, make it to the market. The last one I sold a number of years ago was in GEM condition and fetched $4,200.00. Comparatively, if this large size note came up for sale today, in GEM, it could go under the gavel for more than $100,000 in a highly contested auction.

Artist's impression of a typical Civil War camp-scene, published in Harper's Weekly.

Oh yes, I forgot to warn beginners...collecting fractionals has become more than a hobby. In fractionals, there are many different sizes, colors and denominations. Some are even signed by hand. Some are rated as having only twenty-five extant examples, and others appear only in the Smithsonian Institution in Washington, D.C. Now you would think most of these would be pricey, but as of this writing I can point you to several major bargains still outstanding. Many of these rarities will gain in value in leaps and bounds regardless of condition. Remember, most of these notes disintegrated as they were marched to the battlefield and used until they could no longer be read by the banks. Others remain in large collections, but there are still thousands of collectable examples floating around. And that, my friends, is why we need a new book, one that covers all the bases.

Part One: Introduction

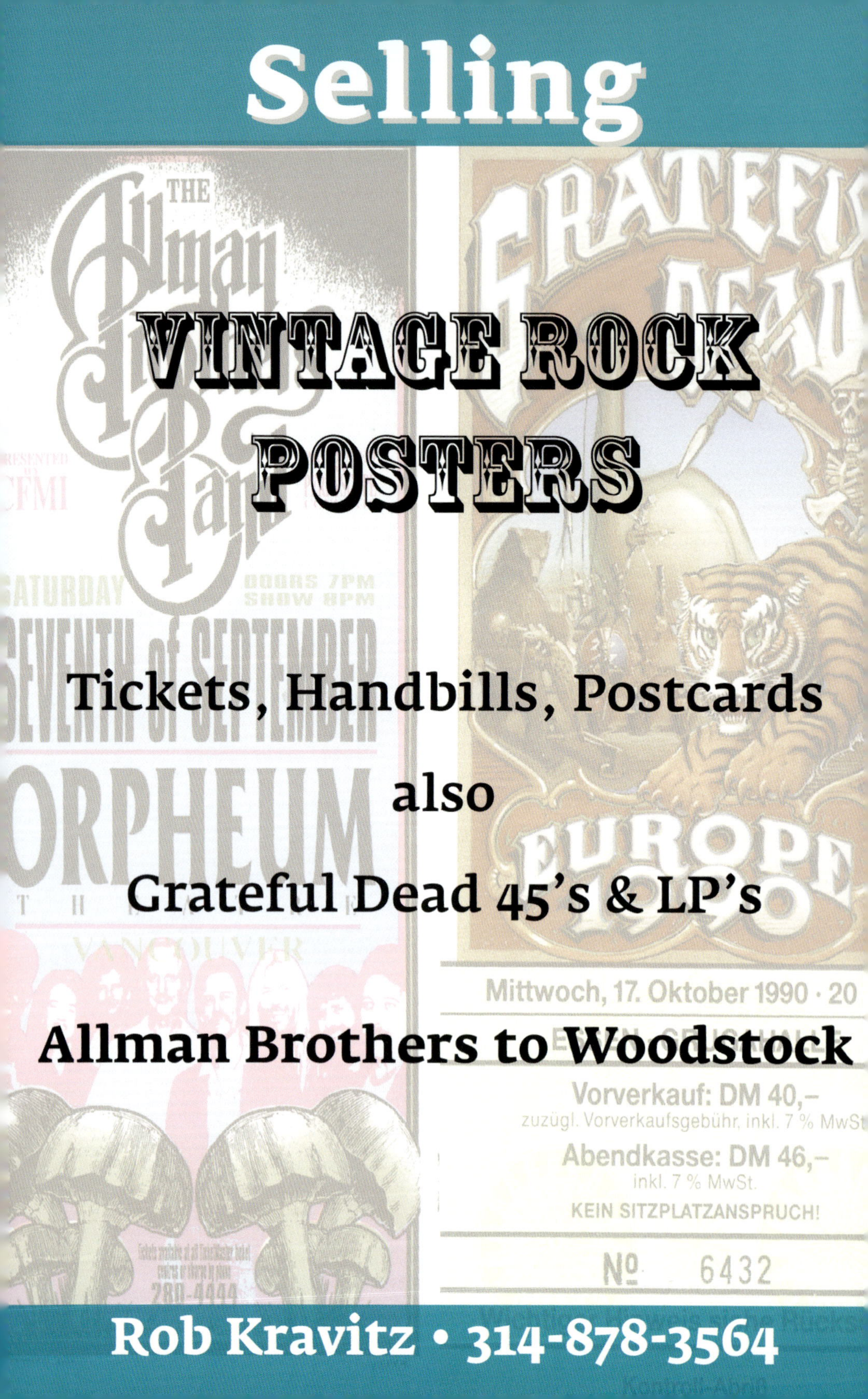
Selling
VINTAGE ROCK POSTERS
Tickets, Handbills, Postcards
also
Grateful Dead 45's & LP's
Allman Brothers to Woodstock
Rob Kravitz • 314-878-3564

I. INTRODUCTION

A COLLECTOR'S GUIDE TO POSTAGE & FRACTIONAL CURRENCY

I designed this to be of use to both novice and expert collectors. In addition, I hope it will shed some light on the history of Fractional Currency in the Civil War era and beyond. The facts contained in it are based on my research and experiences as a fractional currency dealer for over thirty years. The book is also intended to act as an accurate price guide and catalog to the regular issue notes in all the grades, colors and variations.

SLEEPERS

While still in the planning stages I realized there were no books designed to cover those enigmatic notes known as "Sleepers." These are notes which are very tough to find and are usually undervalued, especially in the higher grades. Therefore, I compiled the known data on these and included them as part of a rarity guide for each note.

ERRORS

Every time I attend a show or exhibit I hear a new story about a note containing a mistake that slipped by the printing office. Notes with mistakes in the paper or ink, in the picture or engraving are called "Errors." These notes differ from regular notes in that they may display inverted backs and surcharges or "strange" plate numbers (ie.e mirrored or inverted) all of which tend to make a note very rare and collectable. These errors can be seen in postage stamps and coins as well as paper currency and the value is always higher when an error is encountered. But, when is an error not an error? Unfortunately, many on-line dealers, especially those on eBay, will call a poorly cut note an error when it is nothing more than a misaligned and lower grade note. These subjectively graded notes are of inferior quality and should always go for lower prices.

PRICING

Finally, since no detailed and objective price guide has been published for all eight grades, I've included a comprehensive guide to grading and pricing for use in every day collecting. I have also incorporated a checklist with each note's description. This may be useful in maintaining an inventory of one's collection. The beginner can learn a great deal from this approach and I hope the book will also be trusted by advanced collectors.

PROOFS

Fractional currency is the only field of currency collecting in which proof notes (printed only on one side) are still available-and affordable. They are rare enough to be interesting, and for now, they remain undervalued. For example, there were only 9,016 Grant/Sherman 15¢ specimen notes printed. As of 1884, only 3,513 were still outstanding. How many can there be left today? Were they burned in the Chicago fire? They were printed on a very thin paper, and if mishandled they could disintegrate. Also, many Grant/Sherman notes were hand signed by the treasurers and registers of the United States. Such notes are sure to go up in value, yet most are still very affordable.

GRADING

Grading is a subjective -- hopefully expert -- responsibility and the price of an entire collection can sometimes hinge upon the graders evaluation of a single note. The following grading categories are based on my assessment of industry wide standards used in grading Fractional Currency Notes over the past forty years. These are not arbitrary ideas, pulled from thin air, rather they are values based on the judgments of many collectors and experts. I keep track of all the fractionals I grade by measuring the front margins in millimeters. This technique works best since no two are cut the same and they often have no serial number.

GRADING YOUR NOTES

How do I grade a note? Let's begin with the near impossible. For the first time I am including a discussion of grades above GEM. Occasionally the collector will run into a "dream note" that is perfect in every way. These notes are judged to be so perfect they are called **GEM Plus** or **Above GEM** quality. You may never encounter one of these "babies," but its important to know they exist and how they are graded. Who knows what lurks in grandma's attic?

Even with "high grade" fractionals, only 11% of them turn out to be GEM, also referred to as MS65 (MS stands for Mint State). The grades above GEM, MS66 through MS68, are even more scarce, with perhaps at most 3% qualifying. In the ultra rare category we have MS68 which accounts for 1% or less of the total specimens known. Therefore, approximately 14% of the high quality notes sent for grading are rated GEM or above.

On notes that grade above GEM, it is up to the buyer to determine if that note is worth the asking price as these can range from 150% of GEM to 200% of average GEM prices. I repeat, only you can decide if the premium price is worth it for your collection.

The grades we use to distinguish notes range as follows:

GEM crisp uncirculated (GEM): An almost perfect note. Better than average margins with good centering on both sides for that type of note. Any GEM rating will be tough to obtain because of the margin problems. Most notes were cut by hand with scissors so perfect margins are rare. GEM notes are typically close to the margins and the margins are straight and even. Check your margins first. The note may look great but will be demoted due to this uneven margin problem.

Choice crisp uncirculated (CHCU): A new note, but not quite GEM centering. May be a little off (i.e. three good margins and one close margin.) Might show very slight aging.

Crisp uncirculated (CU): No signs of circulation. Can have centering problems, pin holes, counting mudges or wrinkles, but must have no signs of release to the public or extensive handling.

Almost Uncirculated (AU): These notes will be much like new notes, except for one fold or a couple of corner tip folds.

Extra fine (XF): Circulated. Will have two or three folds and may show signs of gentle handling, but no dirt or grime.

Very fine (VF): Lightly circulated. Will have four to six folds and signs of normal wear, but all other aspects of the note show clearly. The numbers are clear and the ink and registration is clearly visible.

Fine (F): Well circulated, with several folds.

Very good (VG): Will be significantly worn, may be soiled, might have roughness around edges and tears.

WHAT TO LOOK FOR

Experts have several ways of sorting a good note from one of less integrity. The following variables are most often considered by professional graders.

CENTERING

A well focused printing process, also called Centering is very important. If a note has good centering it will be more valuable and more desirable than one that is out of registration. Using the GEM criteria as a judging standard, you can easily see that a note which seems perfect on the front, but has bad margins on the back, will not be GEM. The rear margins may run too close to one side or they may slice slightly away from vertical. In this case both sides need to conform to a center target to meet the GEM criteria.

COLOR

There is only one term that can describe good color in a fractional note, "Freshness." If a note looks bright and unfaded to the naked eye it can grade higher because the color has maintained fresh for more than one hundred years, and that's pretty fresh. Fresh color automatically means the note has not been handled and was stored in ideal conditions, not too hot, not too cold or damp. These are conditions one might find in a bank vault, for example. I have included a color section in this edition to help determine color on a few exemplary and high-grade notes.

PERFORATIONS

Perforations on first issue notes are important. We only see them on the older first issues. These notes were released with perforations on the edges where they were issued in sheets and torn apart like stamps. Perforated notes, to meet the highest standards, must not only have good centering on both sides, but must have **FULL** and clean perforations. Sometimes the perforations are pulled, clipped or trimmed off. Here again you must know which issues had perforations in the first place. In this case you are looking for what is missing rather than any obvious imperfection.

PROCESSED NOTES

Look out for modified notes and notes that may have been tampered with. This is called "processing" and it's a no-no. These "tweaked" and "messed-with" notes have always been around, but I have seen more of them, from more collectors, lately. Some collectors attempt to clean or press notes to make them appear a grade or two better. This is unethical, and can result in damaging the note. In my opinion, once a note falls below a certain grade it can't be upgraded no matter what you do because any "improvements" in one element will probably take away from the original color or some other factor, at least to the expert eye. If you are not sure about the note, do not buy it!

The Army of the Potomac, the Picket Guard. Probably printed originally in Harper's Weekly.

Detecting a Processed Note: Always look carefully at the notes before you buy. Don't buy a choice note unless you absolutely trust your dealer or can examine it in person. Processing comes in many forms. Notes can be cleaned with simply bar soap or bleached. Wrinkles and folds can be pressed or ironed out, pinholes can be filled in and tears can be mended with glue.

Bleaching, starching and pressing notes can actually raise the grade of a note, at least for an amateur grader, but you cannot completely get rid of the cleaning agent. Bleach and chemicals will leave a residue in the paper fibers and mucilage or other glues will show up under magnification. All these practices are detectable with the sniff test. A good nose is invaluable here. If the note smells like bleach it's probably a processed note.

The First U.S. Ironclad, Known as the "St. Louis" or the "Baron de Kalb", launched Oct. 12th, 1861 with an armament of 13 guns.

I have commonly seen notes that have been pressed with a steam or flat iron. This is kind of dumb since the note looks tampered with to a well-trained eye, but people still do it. Sometimes ironing makes the note look uncirculated, but there are ways of detecting pressed notes. Many of the people who iron their notes press only one end to flatten a small fold or short wrinkle or crease, but it looks fake by comparison to the other areas of the same note. The crease is still there, its just less obvious. The crease rarely comes out completely and a deeper look with a magnifier will reveal the old fold.

The Lightbulb Test: Examine the note by holding it up to a good light source at a 45° angle. Move it back and forth to let the light shimmer off the note. Do this on both sides and turn it around to examine it from both ends. The flattened areas or lines (known as artifacts) will cast a shadow and you will see them clearly. Pressed out folds usually show up with shiny lines or cast shadows where the folds once were.

The Curl Test: Lay the note on a clean, dry, flat surface. If the note curls up on the ends, it has probably been processed, or at least washed. It didn't come from the factory that way.

Embossing: Embossing is a method of raising lettering by pressing paper with a special die during the printing process. Many third through fifth issue notes have some degree of embossing on them and most examples are fairly clear. You should be suspicious of processing if this embossing is not apparent. If only half of the note is embossed, be wary of it. Also, as we shall see later, many notes were printed on stronger fiber paper and they should appear thicker than their earlier counterparts. This will be discussed in detail when we look at paper types and the various historical issues.

Ethics: In my opinion, if a note is bleached, cleaned or processed in any way, it is permanently damaged. Some hobbyists think they are preserving the notes by cleaning them, but that's like stripping an original finish from an antique chair... you destroy the real value of any antique when you modify it. Everyone has seen this demonstrated on the PBS program Antique Roadshow.

GUIDE TO RARITY

Grading is based on the condition of a given note, but rarity is a statistical term dealing with how many notes are available to the entire collector pool (i.e. how many notes are deemed to exist by experts in the field). This is determined by consensus and by analysis of government records.

I have included a scarcity and rarity index with each table in the later part of this book. As each note type is presented you will see a rarity rating in the right most column, but for now I think we need a simply definition. The following is a list of terms collectors use to discuss the rarity and commonality of a given note compared to its "family" or issue type. Reading this list over several times will help the new collector gain a feel for the value of the notes.

Very Common: These are the easiest fractionals to find. Not only should you be able to find these at all coin and currency shows, but you will find these notes even at flea markets and antique stores.

Common: You should be able to find these notes at most coin and currency shows and reputable shops.

Scarce: You will find some of these at most coin and currency shows, with a better chance of finding them at the larger shows.

Very Scarce: You might only find these notes at the very large coin and currency shows or at the paper money shows like the ones in Memphis or Chicago.

Rare: Only twenty to thirty notes are known to have survived the past century. Most of the time, you have to wait for one to turn up at a major auction. A dealer who specializes in Fractional Currency would also be a good bet.

Very Rare: Less than twenty known. Again, these usually only show up in major currency auctions, only once in a purple moon would a dealer have one in stock.

Unique: Only one known. Found only in a major auction and museums. Obviously the more unique a note the more valuable it will be, depending on condition.

VALUATIONS

Evaluations are made by human beings and everybody has an opinion. We try to be objective, but sometimes subjective likes and dislikes creep in. Generally, pricing is based on retail prices and/or auction prices realized at the last sale. This variable changes daily, but can usually be extrapolated via the Internet or newsletters and magazines. Prices throughout this book apply to single examples. Evaluations by experts should reflect retail prices over the last ten years, not wholesale. Wholesale trades vary widely and sometimes WILDLY when a good prospect hits the auctions. But the multi-item nature of some of these deals, especially when dealing in whole collections, can hardly be thought of as a stable price platform. You can always try to deal wholesale and get a discount, but retail prices set the standard.

HAND SIGNED NOTES

Yes. you heard me... some of these notes are actually signed by hand. It's hard to imagine an important official sitting around dipping a pen in an ink well 5,000 times, but that's exactly what happened in several cases. This will be covered in more detail in the historical section, but now we need to learn how to identify a signed note.

Almost all hand-signed signatures show a brownish tinge. There

is, most of the time, a noticeable contract between the dark brown and the dark, jet-black ink of the regular printing. The engraved signatures all have a uniform color.The hand-signed notes will always show variations of light and heavy ink. When a line crosses over another, it will always be thicker and darker at the intersection of the two lines. When you turn the note over on a hand-signed note, you will be able to see the signatures from the back of the note. Sometimes light, sometimes dark. This will depend on how much of the ink soaked into the paper.

Also, due to the acid in the inks used for the hand-signed notes, some cracking or burning through the paper may occur. This tends to lower the value and grade of the note.

FINAL WARNING

These terms will become more familiar as you go through this book, but for now, just remember to keep an eye out for processing. Processed notes show up everywhere, from internet auction sites to reputable dealers and collectors. Look over each note you plan to buy very carefully. Fractionals are such a specialized subset of the paper money hobby that many dealers and auctions houses don't pay a lot of attention to them. Potentially, all notes are subject to processing. Most that I have seen are mid-priced ($200.00 to $300.00), although I have seen some of the very rare notes processed.

If you buy a note on the internet or via mail and, after careful scrutiny, find that it has been processed, or is not at the grade advertised, return it for a full refund. All dealers should take back any suspicious notes for a full refund. In my experience no sale is final until the customer is satisfied.

Part Two: History

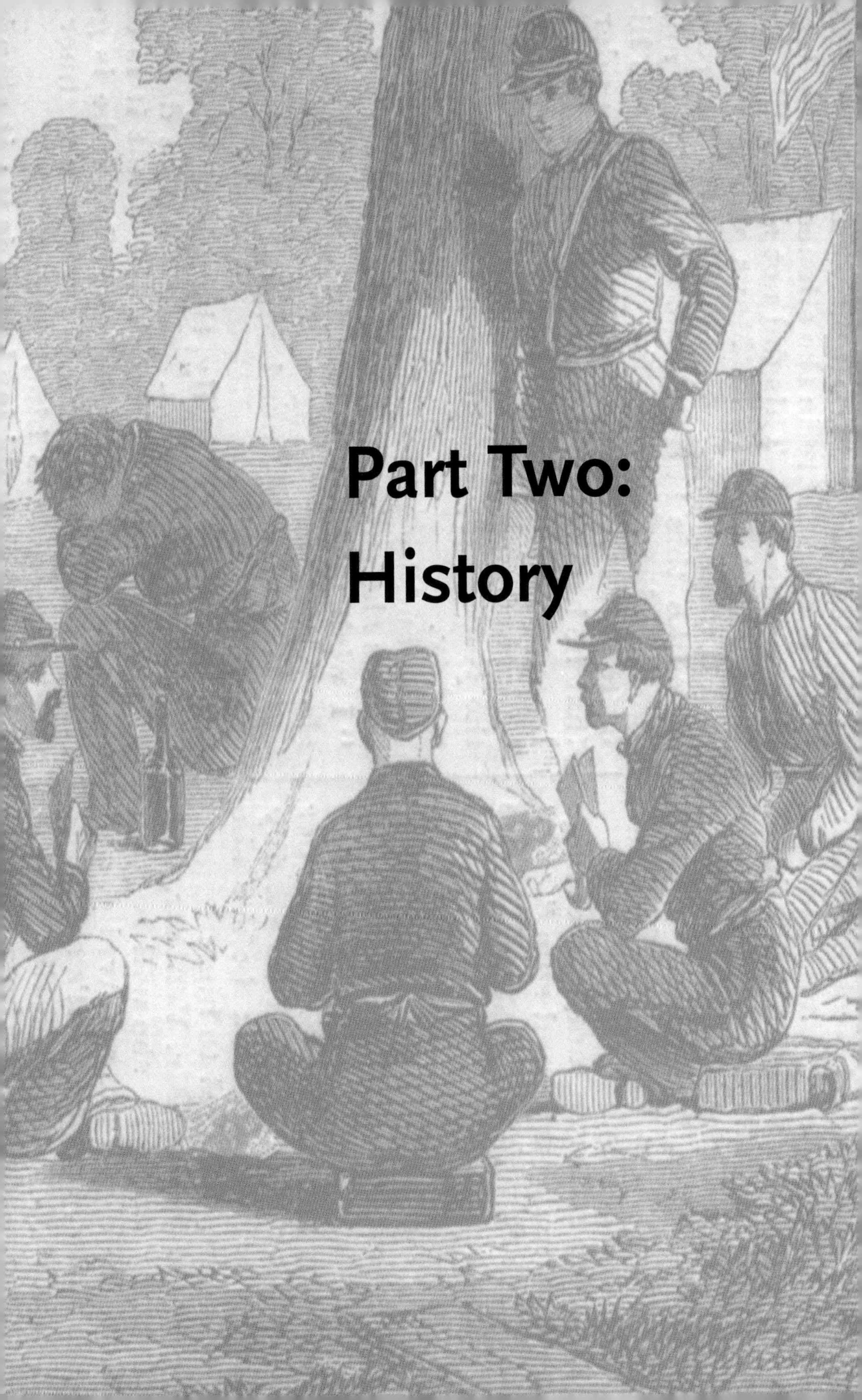

HISTORY

THE POCKET CHANGE OF THE UNION SOLDIER

In the years just before the Civil War, army privates were paid \$11.00 per month, on average. By the end of the war, the same soldier's pay was increased to \$16.00 per month, but this did not keep up with "inflation" and the increases in the cost of goods and services in the civilian world.

In 1860, before the war, boarding houses charged about \$1.75 per week. That's typically two meals a day and a shared room. By 1865, they were charging \$4.00 per week. The price had more than doubled. In 1860, a six room family house in Cincinnati could rent for \$8.00 per month. The rent on the same house had risen to \$25.00 per month by 1865, more than a threefold increase.

In 1861, the New York City banks suspended specie payments (redeeming paper money for silver, gold or copper). Soon, all types of coins vanished from circulation. Copper, silver and gold became worth more than their face value and people started to panic and horde any and all metal coins.

Private individuals started issuing penny sized coins on tokens (Civil War tokens) made of copper or bronze. Cities, banks and merchants also printed and circulated their own private, small notes.

In the early spring of 1862, people in various east coast cities, began using postage stamps as currency (or change). The stamps quickly became sticky and dirty and unfit for postal use, so they became a liability rather than a boost to the economy. Moreover, the practice of turning stamps into money, forced post offices from Washington, D.C., to Boston, to run out of stamps for normal postal use.

Other increases put pressure on the economy. Increases, especially for provisions, staples and commodities, were drastic between 1860 and 1865. Beef steaks more than doubled in price, from 12¢ to 30¢ per pound. Raw wheat flour went from $8.25 to $15.50 per barrel while sugar and coffee rose from 8¢ to 12¢ and finally to 35¢ per pound.

Earnings seemed to increase, but not equally. The war effort put a demand on industries that manufactured items such as blankets and boots. A blacksmith, earning $1.81 per day in 1860, was bringing home $2.88 by 1865. Similarly, masons wages rose from $1.98 to $2.91 per day during the same period, you do the math, that's a lot of money, but school teachers salaries and self-employed income stayed the same or went up only slightly during those troubled years.

These are images taken from CivilWar era patriotic envelopes.

Top: Kimmel Patriots flag, shield andeagle in black;

Below: multi-colored eagle and shield;

Next Page: multi-colored standing Liberty.

THE FIRST FRACTONAL NOTES

The introduction of Fractional Currency was critical to the economy of the North both during the Civil War, and for years thereafter. It eased stress in many economic areas and it helped to abate poverty, because cash was flowing again. More directly, Fractional Currency helped finance the war with $368,724,079.45 being issued for the Northern interests.

One answer to the coin shortage was invented by John Gault, a private business man, who patented a round brass case to go around a postage stamp, to protect it from deterioration.

Gault put advertisements on the backs of the coin cases. This worked for awhile, but they proved impractical because the mica window on the center of the case used to show the denomination of the stamp cracked. In addition many people took offense to the advertising.

"Good try, but no Cigar," the newspapers wagged. Gault's encased postage stamp idea appears to have been too little, too late for several economic reasons. First, they circulated in far too small a quantity to relieve the money shortage and they, again, ate up the inventory of actual postage stamps, making it difficult to mail a post card or letter. The country was already short on stamps, and, for a few months nothing else was available, except small private issue notes that could only be redeemed by the issuing party, almost like a gift certificate today. This could clearly lead to all manner of mischief. It was as if anybody with a printing press could issue money.

The Treasurer of the United States, General Francis E. Spinner, decided to do something before the crisis grew worse. He pasted a few postage stamps to rectangles of Treasury Department marked paper in definite amounts, 5¢, 10¢, 25¢ and 50¢. He then signed some of them so that they would be harder to duplicate.

The idea caught on with Congress mainly because the paper he used was tougher than the stamps. Again this was only an interim solution, but it showed the way for future changes. The definite value and convenience of the "notes" as arranged by General Spinner, was readily apparent.

Congress was impressed as the need for a permanent solution became more critical. A small change substitute law was proposed and, in the summer of 1862, the Postage Currency Bill became law. This law was officially signed by President Lincoln on July 17, 1862. The law forbade any further notes below $1.00 face value to be issued by private companies, banks or individuals with a penalty of up to six months in jail, or a $200.00 fine for each offense.

ORDER OF ISSUE AT-A-GLANCE

Later I will discuss the various issues in detail, but for now the date of issue and history of each note is extremely important and the order of issue carries with it a great deal of information for the collector. Memorizing the dates the notes were issued is a great way to memorize the entire world of Fractional Currency. According to government records the true order of issue for Fractional Currency in each denomination is as follows:

FIRST ISSUE

5¢ First Issue note

The first coin substitute notes issued under the 1862 Act were called Postage Currency. These notes are easily identified because they feature reproductions of the then current postage stamps. The 5¢ notes featured a single five-cent stamp with the portrait of Thomas Jefferson on the face, while the 25¢ note features the same stamp reproduced five times. The 10¢ note shows a single ten-cent stamp with George Washington's portrait. The 50¢ note features the same Washington stamp reproduced five times. The notes interestingly enough, also came with both perforated and straight edges. They were printed by the American Bank Note Company (ABNC) and the National Bank Note Company (NBNC) which were basically extensions of the government holding a special license amounting to a monopoly.

SECOND ISSUE

With the Act of July 11, 1863, the Treasury Department started to print its own notes. All second issue notes were printed at the Treasury Department. The second issue notes came about because the Union government wanted to move away from the use of the postage stamp metaphor while keeping a sense of patriotism intact. All the notes have the portrait of George Washington on the front with a bronze oval surcharge around the portrait. All the fronts of the notes regardless of denomination, are all gray-slate colored. The backs are in the following colors: 5¢ note: tan to brown; 10¢ note: light to dark green; 25¢ note: violet to purple; and the 50¢ note: reddish-orange to red. The backs also have their denomination on them in a large bronze numerical surcharge overprint.

5¢ Second Issue note

THIRD ISSUE

The third issue of Fractional Currency started at the end of 1864 with the war going full blast. As the quality of the Fractional Notes improved, so did the quality of the counterfeits of the earlier issue notes. This, and the ever-increasing demand for "small change," made a design change necessary.

There are more varieties of notes in the third issue than the other issues combined. The third issue started signatures on the notes, some printed and some autographed. These are red and green backs, plain paper and fiber paper, different surcharges and different sheet positions indicators. All this helps to account for nineteen different 50¢ Spinner notes, and thirty two different 50¢ Justice notes. This also is the only issue to have 3¢ notes.

5¢ Third Issue note

FOURTH ISSUE

10¢ Fourth Issue note

Improvements to quality and anticounterfeiting continued for ten years with the fourth and fifth issues of Fractional Currency. One anti-counterfeiting measure included the addition of the Treasury Seal on the front of each note. Another was adding blue fibers to the right side of the notes. All the notes have printed signatures for added security. These anti-counterfeiting measures worked to varying degrees. But they did not stop counterfeiting altogether. The 50¢ Lincoln and the 50¢ Stanton were both counterfeited as soon as they came out. The last note of the fourth issue was the 50¢ Dexter but it too, was soon counterfeited. As the war ended a cure for this counterfeiting had to be developed, so a new bill was passed.

FIFTH ISSUE

10¢ Fifth Issue note

The Currency Act of April 17, 1876, directed that all Fractional Currency notes were to be redeemable with silver coin. This act also brought about the fifth issue of fractional paper that was not as easy to fake.

The fifth, and last, issue used only 10¢, 25¢ and 50¢ notes. There are just a few varieties: the 10¢ green seal; the 10¢ red seal with "short and long key"; and the 25¢ notes also with red seals and "short and long keys." These terms will be defined later on. Basically these notes have green backs with the fronts printed in black.

ISSUE DETAILS

Let's take a look at the notes in more detail, this time using the traditional Friedberg catalog numbers.

FIRST ISSUE

First issue notes were released between August 21, 1862 and May 29, 1863. These were trimmed by hand, but production was slow so the notes were treated more like stamps. They came on large perforated sheets mostly to ease the job of separating and trimming each note. Some of these sheets still exist and are highly collectable, just like stamp sheets with serial numbers.

Unfortunately the perforation idea proved less than ideal. Perforated stamps are designed to use once and once only. The buyer moistens the back, pastes it down and mails the letter or card. But fractional notes had a tougher row to hoe. The sheets themselves came apart in shipping. Moreover the notes were much larger and heavier than stamps and even with special handling, many were damaged before they got into circulation. Perforating was stopped almost immediately in favor of the straight edge. This accounts, at least in part, for the rarity of the perforated notes.

The fact that various production techniques were tried allows an order of issue for these historically important slips of paper. Most experts agree that the first issue notes came out in the following sequence:

- Straight Edge Hand cut with no monogram
- Perforated with no monogram
- Perforated with ABNCo monogram
- Straight Edged with ABNCo monogram

The Battle of Champion's Hilll, May 16, 1863. Sketched by Mr. Theodore R. Davis.

Reproduced from Harper's Weekly, June 20, 1863

SECOND ISSUE

The massive second issue, released between October 10, 1863 to February 23, 1867, was printed in four denominations. All four values, 5¢, 10¢, 25¢ and 50¢, have the same design with variations in color, paper type and surcharge. The front of each note shows the portrait of Washington and the background is a dock scene engraved by James Duthie from the Currency Bureau. The back of each note is an eagle atop a shield containing the corresponding denomination numeral.

Dock scene engraved by James Duthie for the front of the second issue notes.

Bronze Ovals

A unique feature of the second issue notes was the bronze oval that surrounded the portrait of Washington on the front of the notes. The bronze was also used to print the surcharges on the back of the notes.

The bronze was designed to prevent counterfeiters from making photographs of the real notes, and in turn, use the photos to make printing plates. Photographic film at the time could not pick up the design printed on top of the bronze. So therefore they could not make a good copy that way. At first glance it looks like the bronze is over the printing, but under 30X magnification you can tell the printing is over the bronze oval.

This process was the idea of Spencer M. Clark who was well pleased with his invention. He described the bronzing feature as having "defied all the attempts of the Scientific Commission to successfully remove it." He further stated that he had never seen a piece of paper from which it had been removed without also removing the engraving.

The backs also vary in color as follows:

- 5¢ notes are brown
- 10¢ notes are light to dark green
- 25¢ notes are light to dark purple
- 50¢ notes are light to dark red

The backs of the notes may also display surcharges.

Note: The numbers associated with the following descriptions relate to catalog designations for specific identification. These are shown in parenthesis with the letters "Fr" followed by a number. This catalog typology will be explained fully in the next major section. As stated above, the Fr. stands for Friedberg, named after Robert Friedberg, who designed the numbering system now commonly used.

A Note on Paper Types: At least eleven different experimental papers were used in, mostly vain, attempts to stop counterfeiting. The notes of the second issue notes to be printed were produced on "membrane," now known as fiber paper. The fiber looked promising but failed miserably in the field. These sheets were actually sandwiches of thin paper bonded together with scattered long fibers. One would think they might serve to stop the criminal element, but alas, once the secret was out the paper was easily duplicated and the layers tended to pull apart. This helps account for the rarity of the fiber paper notes.

RARE "TREASURY RECTANGLES"

A lot of the first issue notes were counterfeited. Therefore a concerned Congress ordered the Treasury Department to print notes on distinctive paper. They had no distinctive paper at the time and were pressed for time to start printing the second issue notes.

By taking regular bank note paper and imprinting it with a rectangular treasury stamp ( ) and making it Treasury paper, therefore making it a distinctive paper.

The rectangle was at the very edge of the sheet and it was intended to be trimmed off when the sheets were cut, which accounts for it's rarity! These are found only on the second issue notes.

The following are how many that are known:

- Fr. 1232 - One full sheet with seal on lower right bottom corner (ex: Rockholt/Milt Friedberg)
- Fr. 1232 5¢ notes - 6 known
- Fr. 1244 10¢ notes - 10 known
- Fr. 1283 25¢ notes - 15 known
- Fr. 1316 50¢ notes - none known

FIVE CENT SECOND ISSUE

Some fifty-six million, 5¢ second issue notes were issued between October 10, 1863 through March 1, 1865. As the war ended most were issued on bank note paper.

The first 5¢ notes were issued during the war, were printed on Dr. Gwynn's fiber paper with R-1-18-63 surcharges on the back corners. These bear a catalog number of Fr. 1235. Although printing was suspended, only 12,000 (11,837 to be exact) were issued. These were continuously released over the next year ending through October of 1864.

The next 5¢ note, Fr. 1234 came out with the 𝔖-18-63 surcharge. The Fr. 1233 looks identical but is surcharge with just 18-63. The last 5¢ notes to be made were the Fr. 1232, which has no surcharge on the back except for a large bronze "5".

TEN CENT SECOND ISSUE

Of the 10¢ notes, some 61,760,843 were issued between October 10, 1863 and March, 1865. Persisting in the use of fiber paper for the notes, the Fr. 1249 examples were released with the back corners surcharge of 𝔗-1-18-63. Only 17,098 were issued through October 1, 1863.

The next 10¢ note, the first on regular bank paper, is the Fr. 1248, surcharged 𝔒-63 on the upper back corners. All but one of the twenty examples known have the plain O-63 surcharge style. The one that sold in the March 17, 1993 Halpern sale is the only known example. The Halpern sale item has an ornate 𝔒-63 surcharge, the only ornate style known. This is similar to the remaining surcharges on all of the other second issue notes. It is my opinion, and that of others, that this is the only "genuine" example of this note. Many of the major collectors over the years, e.g. F.C.C. Boyd, W. Raymond and Matt Rothert, erroneously collected the "non-genuine" 𝔒-63. Which begs the question: What happened to the other notes?

The next 10¢ note that was issued was the Fr. 1247 "1" in the upper right hand corner, and "18"-"63" on the lower back corners.

The Fr. 1246 could have been next, with "𝔖" in the upper left corner, and "18"-"63" on the lower back corners. Several notes have been seen with the "𝔖" inverted, but have not been given an Fr. Catalog number.

Both the Fr. 1245 with "18"-"63" on the lower back corners and the Fr. 1244 with no surcharges were issued in huge numbers.

TWENTY FIVE CENT SECOND ISSUE

Of the 25¢ second issue notes, some 30,593,365 were issued. Again, the first to be printed were the fiber paper notes, but, as usual, they are scarce. Only 58,689 of these were issued from October, 1863 through October, 1864.

Two types of 25¢ fiber notes are known with separate catalog numbers. The Fr. 1289 has a surcharge of "𝔗-1-18-63" and the Fr. 1290 shows a surcharge of "𝔗-2-18-63".

Walter Breen—widely considered one of the foremost numismatic historians and researchers—believed that the "𝔗" must stand for a particular type of printing process, -1 for wet printing, and 𝕿-2 for dry printing. If he is correct, we can catch a glimpse of the experimental printing process that went on 150 years ago.

The next 25¢ notes to be printed were issued on regular bank note paper. These are: Fr. 1288 surcharged "2-18-63"; Fr. 1286, surcharged "𝕾-18-63"; Fr. 1285, surcharged "𝕬-18-63"; Fr. 1284, surcharged with just "18-63", and lastly, Fr. 1283, without any surcharge.

FIFTY CENT SECOND ISSUE

More than twelve million 50¢ second issue notes were released. Of these, a small number, some 62,300, were fiber notes, issued through October 1, 1864.

The three fiber paper 50¢ notes are: Fr. 1320 with surcharges "𝕺-1-18-63" on the corners of the back; Fr. 1321, with surcharges "𝕽-2-18-63"; and the most common of the three (it any fiber note can be called common) is the Fr. 1322 with surcharges "𝕿-1-18-63".

The remaining 50¢ notes in the second printing came out on regular bank note paper. They are as follows: Fr. 1318 with surcharges "1-18-63" on the corners of the back; Fr. 1316 with just "18-63" on the lower back corners. A Fr.1314 with no surcharges is rumored to exist, but I have never seen one that was not made by erasing the surcharges. The real Fr. 1314 only exists in specimen form.

THIRD ISSUE

The third issue of Fractional Currency was issued to the public from December 5, 1864, to August 16, 1869. It came in five denominations. The 5¢, 10¢, 25¢, and 50¢ notes of the second issue were continued, but a new 3¢ denomination was added. Some of the third issue notes were printed on left over fiber paper from the second issue. Third issue notes were printed from December 5, 1864 (experimental, fiber paper 50¢ note) through April 15, 1869.

THREE CENT THIRD ISSUE

The 3¢ note is the only third issue note without signatures. More than twenty million were issued from January 23rd, to April 5, 1865. More importantly, they represent the only 3 cent notes in fractional currency. They were issued in keeping with the Congressional Act of March 3, 1865, which authorized release of 3¢ metal coins (ironically these were struck in nickel) and, for the first time, the redemption of 3¢ Fractional currency notes for the new, 3¢ nickel coin.

There are two major types of 3¢ notes, the Fr. 1226 with light black background behind the portrait of George Washington, and the Fr. 1227 which has a dark background. This latter note was made from only seven face plates which makes it much rarer than the Fr. 1226 which was made from thirty three face plates.

FIVE CENT THIRD ISSUE

The third issue 5¢ notes were printed at the end of the war, between January, 1865 to sometime in April, 1866. About 13 million were authorized and issued. These are very collectible and controversial notes, and need to be discussed in detail, mainly because Spencer Clark decided to put his own face on the note instead of that of explorer William Clark. By so doing he outraged Congress who promptly enacted a law banning the portrait of any living person on U.S. Currency. This law is still on the books and extends also to stamps. For a detailed account, see Spencer Clark's biography in the section "Faces on the notes."

Despite the new law, the controversial notes continue to be issued for the next two years afterward. Notes on the far left of the sheets had a position letter "a" on them. There are two major varieties: Red Back and Green Back notes.

The four different 5¢ notes are:

- Fr. 1236, Red Back
- Fr. 1237, Red Back with Position Letter "a" on the front
- Fr. 1238, Green Back
- Fr. 1239, Green Back with position letter "a" on the front

By the end of June, 1884, some 10.4 million 5¢ notes had been redeemed for silver coins, leaving over 2.5 million still outstanding at war's end. These, and the 10¢ notes described next, are fairly easy to pick up at auction sales and in shops, but again condition means a great deal.

TEN CENT THIRD ISSUE

Over 150 million, Third Issue 10¢ notes, were printed but only 18,000 Red Backs were issued between August 25, and September 9, 1865, and only a small fraction of that run were autographed.

The autographed notes are as follows: Fr. 1253 with autograph signatures of Colby and Spinner, and the much scarcer, Fr. 1254 with autographed signatures of Jeffries and Spinner. Next printed were the Fr. 1251 and Fr. 1252 Red Backs with printed signatures

The Fr. 1255A with the autographed signatures of Colby and Spinner, is unlike all the rest of the autographed notes, because it has a green back. This has to be considered a major error, rather than a regularly printed note and was probably a presentation piece. It's what is known as a "mule error" in that the wrong back was used after the normal issues of Red Backs were stopped.

Next to be issued were the regular Green Back notes as follows: Fr. 1255, with no position indicator; and Fr. 1256, with position indicator "1" on the front.

Also worth noting is the fact that the 10¢ notes lacked the word "cents" anywhere on them, so it is safe to assume that many could have been passed as $10 notes.

TWENTY FIVE CENT THIRD ISSUE

Of the 25¢ Third Issue notes, 123,572,755 were printed through April 15, 1869. These notes portray William Fessenden, who , at the time, was still alive. One wonders how this could have happened after the law of April, 1866, forbade portraying a living person on currency, but exceptions were made.

The first to be printed were the 16,000 Red Backs, printed and issued from February 21, through March 6, 1866. They are as follows:

- Fr. 1291, with no position indicator.
- Fr. 1292, with position indicator "a"

The first of the Green Back notes were printed on fiber paper, with surcharges "M-2-6-5". Only 7,107 notes were printed and issued on March 22, 1965. The very first few sheets were on fragile fiber paper. Most of the notes that have survived show missing corners and heavy cracked center folds. These are the famous, solid bronze front surcharges:

- Fr. 1299, with no position indicator
- Fr. 1300, with position indicator "a" - very rare

Because of its poor wearing quality, use of this fragile fiber paper was stopped immediately, which is partly why these notes are so rare. Again, this is one of the eleven known experimental papers used in fractionals during the war.

The next fiber paper used was more durable and all of the notes printed on it had a back surcharge "M-2-6-5". These are:

- Fr. 1297, with no position indicator
- Fr. 1298, with position indicator "a"

As usual, the Green Back notes on regular bank note paper came out only after several fragile papers were used. They are:

- Fr. 1294, with no position indicator
- Fr. 1295, with position indicator "a"
- Fr. 1296, with position indicator "a" 7mm down and to the right of the normal location

Also, the "a" is larger on the Fr. 1296 note. In this case, the letter "a" is 2mm in size, whereas the normal "a" is 1mm in size. Only 16 or so of these are known today.

FIFTY CENT - THIRD ISSUE - JUSTICE NOTES

Justice notes are named for the vignette on the front depicting Lady Justice holding her scales in balance. Her appearance on fifty cent third issue and specimen notes differentiates a Justice note from a Spinner note of the same denomination. In all, 73,471,853 notes of all types were printed and released.

The first Justice notes were released on December 5, 1864 with almost 10 million printed. But there were two other types printed in the 50¢ denomination. The Spinner type I back was produced in a run of 52,866,690 while the Spinner Type II back came out in a much smaller edition of 10,886,028.

All three types were printed in sheets of twelve. The notes on the far left column of the sheet each have the position indicator "1", and the top row of the sheet have position indicator "a". So there is only one note out of the twelve that has both the "1" and "a" position indicators. This makes that single note more scarce than the other eleven notes on the sheet.

The first notes in this series are designated Fr. 1357. These are the first notes depicting "Lady Justice." They are red backed fiber paper notes carrying the autographed signatures of Colby and Spinner. They come with the surcharge "S-2-6-4" on the back. Only 3,060 notes were printed on November 14, 1864. This was, more than likely, an experimental printing. It also seems possible that the very rare Fr. 1351, Fr. 1352, Fr. 1353 and Fr. 1354 could have come from this same printing, since they are also printed on the same fiber paper and have the same surcharges.

These later notes have printed signatures and are not hand signed like the Fr. 1357. The very rare Fr. 1373A was printed on the same type of paper, with the same surcharges and printed signatures, but with a green back. This could also be from the same experimental printing as the Fr. 1357. It is possible that only one sheet was printed, since only nine notes are known today. Each of the nine notes that are now in collections are worth $40,000-$70,000 each depending on condition.

Several other fiber paper "Justice" notes have green backs with a surcharge of "A-2-6-5". Fr. 1370, has no position indicators. Fr. 1371, (which is very rare) displays position indicators "1" and "a" on the front.

Justice note variations are as follows:

- Fr. 1372, Position indicator "1"
- Fr. 1373, position indicator "a"

The next series of Justice notes released were all Red Backs:

- Fr. 1343, with no surcharges
- Fr. 1344, position indicators "1" and "a" - rare
- Fr. 1345, position indicator "1"
- Fr. 1346, position indicator "a", surcharge "A-2-6-5" on back
- Fr. 1347, no position indicators
- Fr. 1348, position indicators "1" and "a" - very rare
- Fr. 1349, position indicator "1"
- Fr. 1350, position indicator "a"
- Fr. 1355, hand signed, no surcharge on back
- Fr. 1356, hand signed with surcharge "A-2-6-5" on back.

The following numbers are Green Back notes:

- Fr. 1358, no position indicators
- Fr. 1359, position indicators "1" and "a" - rare note with 30 known
- Fr. 1360, position indicator "1"
- Fr. 1361, position indicator "a"
- Fr. 1362, no position indicators, surcharge "A-2-6-5" compactly spaced 92mm x 30mm on back
- Fr. 1363, position indicators "1" and "a"
- Fr. 1364, position indicator "1"
- Fr. 1365, position indicator "a"

You can also find some Green Backs with surcharge "A-2-6-5" widely spaced 98mm x 34mm. These are:

- Fr. 1366, no position indicators
- Fr. 1367, position indicators "1" and "a", this is a very rare note
- Fr. 1368, position indicator "1"
- Fr. 1369, position indicator "a"

FIFTY CENT - THIRD ISSUE - SPINNER NOTES

January 1, 1866 through March 23, 1869 saw the Spinner portrait used for the first time. The Spinner Type I backs are the same design as the Justice note backs. Most of the Spinner notes were not in violation of the "no living person on notes" Act of April 7, 1866 because the plates were made before that date. (See Spencer Clark entry in the Faces on the Notes section.)

Fr. 1328, a red back, was the first of these Spinner notes to be printed. These carried the surcharge "A-2-6-5". Probably only the first few hundred were actually signed by Colby and Spinner.

The Fr. 1329 red backs had the autograph signatures of Allison and Spinner. The Fr. 1330 were signed Allison and New, probably on sheets that Colby didn't sign. This signing must have happened sometime between April 3, and August 15, 1869, since this was the only time that the their terms of office overlapped. Most of the known Fr. 1330 notes are graded uncirculated or better and are now considered to be very valuable.

In his book *A Checking List of Fractional Currency*, Walter Schultz says "B.F. Collins, one of the best-known and foremost numismatists of his time, and for many years employed in the Bureau of Engraving and Printing, is said to be responsible for New's autographing a dozen or so of the blank 50¢ Spinner notes."

The non-signed Spinner red backs are:

- ➢ Fr. 1324, no position indicator
- ➢ Fr. 1325, position indicators "1" and "a"
- ➢ Fr. 1326, position indicator "1"
- ➢ Fr. 1327, position indicator "a"

The Green Back Spinner notes came with and without back corner surcharges. The "Greens" without surcharges are:

- ➢ Fr. 1331, no position indicators
- ➢ Fr. 1332, position indicators "1" and "a"
- ➢ Fr. 1333, position indicator "1"
- ➢ Fr, 1334, position indicator "a"

The Green Backs with surcharges "A-2-6-5" are:

- ➢ Fr. 1335, no position indicators
- ➢ Fr. 1336, position indicators "1" and "a", very rare, less then 20 examples known.
- ➢ Fr. 1337, position indicator "1"
- ➢ Fr. 1338, position indicator "a"

Finally, the Spinner notes with the Type II back and no surcharges were printed between May 27, 1868 and April 15, 1869, with some 10,868,028 notes issued. These notes were the last of the Third Issue. There were only four types of Spinner Type II back issued. They are:

- ➢ Fr. 1339, no position indicators
- ➢ Fr. 1340, position indicators "1" and "a"
- ➢ Fr. 1341, position indicator "1"
- ➢ Fr. 1342, position indicator "a"

FOURTH ISSUE

The fourth issue Fractional Currency notes were released after the war between July 14, 1869 and February 16, 1875 and these are the first notes to display Treasury Seals. All of these notes bear the printed signatures of Allison and Spinner.

Fourth issue notes printed during 1869 have two types of paper. The first group is watermarked: the letters "US" in two rows. The second type, not watermarked, has light to dark red fibers scattered in the paper.

Starting in 1870, a new type of paper was put into use from the Wilcox Paper Co., with what was officially called "localized blue stain", now just called "blue end notes." Starting at the end of 1871, a smaller seal (38mm) replaced the larger (40mm) design.

TEN CENTS FOURTH ISSUE

Some 349,409,600 10¢, fourth issue notes were issued through February 1874, of which 170,312,600 had the small seal. This means, 179,097,000 had the larger seal. There are basically four varieties of the fourth issue 10¢ note. The Fr. 1257 is on watermarked paper with scattered light fibers; the Fr. 1258 has no watermarks and more red than pinkish fibers with some blue or violet scattered throughout. The Fr. 1259 is a blue end, but the blue aspect is sometimes very light and faint. The Fr. 1261 with blue end has a small seal (38mm). The colors of the seals can be from a light rose to a dark burgundy (which sometimes can look brownish). The Fr. 1260 seal is generally considered to have been originally red, but is now referred to as a Brown Seal. This may indicate a change in ink chemistry. This number is no longer in the Friedberg book, but is still collectible.

FIFTEEN CENTS FOURTH ISSUE

Of the 35,361,440 fifteen cent notes issued, 8,121,400 (printed April, 1872 to March, 1874) had the smaller 38mm seal. Varieties are:

- Fr. 1267, watermark "USUSUSUS" with large 40mm seal
- Fr. 1268, no watermark, course paper with reddish fibers and large (40mm) seal (rare and deceivingly easy to mis attribute)
- Fr. 1269, large (40mm) seal with blue end
- Fr. 1270, brownish seal
- Fr. 1271, small (38mm) seal with blue end

TWENTY-FIVE CENTS FOURTH ISSUE

There were 235,689,024 twenty-five cent notes issues with 32,516,256 having the small (38mm) seal. Varieties are:

- Fr. 1301, large seal, watermarked USUSUS

- Fr. 1302, large seal, no watermark
- Fr. 1303, large seal, with blue end
- Fr. 1304, large brown seal, plain paper
- Fr. 1307, small seal with blue end

FIFTY CENTS FOUTH ISSUE

Some 154,799,200 fifty-cent notes were issued, of which 19,152,000 were Fr. 1374 Lincoln notes that were watermarked "USUSUS". These were issued from July, 1869 through December, 1869. The issue of Lincoln notes was stopped and recalled because of the large quantities of very good counterfeits that appeared. From January 1870, through September 1873, 86,048,000 Fr. 1376 Stanton notes were issued. These too, were immediately and aggressively counterfeited, causing yet another note to be issued. The Fr. 1379, this one with the portrait of Samuel Dexter on the face, was printed in a run of 49,599,200 and released from August 3, 1873 through February 16, 1974. This too, was counterfeited.

FIFTH ISSUE

The fifth issue notes were distributed between February 26, 1874 and February 15, 1876. They came in three denominations: 10¢, 25¢ and 50¢. The 10¢ and 25¢ notes had the printed signatures of Allison and Spinner. The 10¢ and 25¢ varieties are marked "Series of 1874" and the 50¢ notes are marked/dated, "Series of 1875". These later notes also carry the printed signatures of Allison and New. All the 50¢ notes are on paper with the localized blue ends.

The 10¢ fifth issue notes came out with the portrait of the recently deceased William Meredith, who was Secretary of the Treasury 1849 through 1850. Notes were issued from July, 1874 to February 15, 1876. A total of 199,899,000 were sent out. The first ones issued, Fr. 1264, have a green Treasury seal with a long, thin 5mm key.

There are two types of the red seals, Fr. 1265, long, thin, 5mmkey, and Fr. 1266, short, thick, 4mm key.

The 25¢ Robert Walker note commemorates the Secretary of the Treasury from 1845 to 1849. They were issued from July, 1874, to February 15, 1876. A total of 144,368,000 were distributed. Like the 10¢ variety, there are two types: Fr. 1308, with a long, thin 5mm key in the Treasury red seal, and Fr. 1309, with a short, thick 4mm key.

The 50¢ Crawford notes were issued from July 1875, through February, 1876 in a printing of 13,160,000.

CAPTURED PAPER

Confederate States of America paper was manufactured in Great Britain for use in making Confederate States paper money. It was used on \$5.00, \$10.00, \$20.00, \$50.00 and \$100.00 notes. The sheets are 13.5 inches by 16 inches. It has eight water marks (CSA in block letters) per sheet. They appear vertically. Blank sheets are still available today anywhere from \$125.00 to \$200.00 per sheet.

During the Civil War, the Confederate States plied a trade route between Wilmington, N.C. and Nassau, Bahamas Islands. They would ship out bales of cotton and bring back much needed ammunition, guns, drugs, paper and other items. The Union government declared a blockade on April 19, 1861, which just about closed all the Confederate ports.

The "Bermuda", a blockade-runner, bringing back Civil War supplies from Liverpool, was sighted in the Atlantic Ocean on April 27, 1862. The United States ship the "Mercedita" captured the "Bermuda" which was taken to a Northern port. It was judged a legal prize of war by a Federal Court, and the cargo ordered sold.

The Treasury Department bought five cases of banknote paper in this sale and immediately put to work. This paper was used to print specimen notes for the second and third issues of Fractional Currency.

WHAT TO LOOK FOR

Due to the size and spacing of the notes on confiscated sheets, only one or two of the C.S.A. watermark letters appear on any one specimen note. It's very unusual to find a note with all three letters.

PUBLIC SPECIMEN SETS

Starting in September, 1867, the Government offered specimen sets for sale to the public. They offered two different sets. One was a full set of regular issued notes, comprising all the varieties and denominations as originally issued from the first three issues of Postage and Fractional Currency, a total of twenty size notes.

The other was a set of "half-notes" (wide margin specimens having the face and the back printed on separate sheets). This set had 34 pieces. Those lucky enough to get a regular issue set in September, got perforated notes (5¢, 10¢, 25¢, and 50¢). Those who got their sets in October, 1867 or later, did not get the perforated notes, but they got a 90¢ refund.

Collectors note: To the best of my knowledge, all but two of the original wide margin specimen sets have been broken up over the years. The only time both sets have been on display was when I displayed them at the Memphis Paper Money show in June, 2001. The display won second place for Fractional Currency. Shortly thereafter, both sets sold to a Northern California collector who will keep both sets in unbroken condition.

FACES ON THE NOTES

After the war began, several leaders and presidents were depicted on stamps and fractional currency. The Civil War President, Secretary of War, Treasurer, and two Civil War heros. appeared as well as Thomas Jefferson and George Washington. Following, in alphabetical order, is a brief biography of each man with special emphasis on his relevance to postage and fractional currency developments.

SPENCER M. CLARK

Born: June 3, 1811. Died: December 10, 1890.

Spencer Clark is perhaps the only antihero ever depicted on Fractional Currency. He appears on the third issue 5¢ note, but this honor is a bit overstated. Clark, the appointed head of the Currency Bureau, put his own portrait on the third issue note instead of the explorer, William Clark, of the Lewis and Clark expeditions. This could hardly have been a mistake and smacked of gross malfeasance as well as contempt of Congress. John Q. Public was also not amused. I guess Clark thought of it as a practical joke, but Congress didn't agree and his blasphemous act, especially in time of war and national crisis, did not go unpunished. Clark's vanity so incensed the Congress, they were moved to enact the Act of April 7, 1866, which banned the portrayal of living persons on any U.S. Currency, stamps or bonds. This law is still in effect. Interestingly enough, about a month later, on May 9 and 10, 1866, Clark presented currency specimen books (now known as Presentation Books) to President Andrew Johnson, Chief Justice Chase, Treasurer Spinner and other Cabinet members. Was this to apologize for putting his own face on the 5¢ note? If so, it didn't work. Clark was censured anyway.

WILLIAM HARRIS CRAWFORD

Born: February 24, 1772. Died: September 15, 1834.

William H. Crawford's portrait is on the 50¢ fifth issue notes. He was admitted to the bar in 1798. Mr. Crawford was elected to Georgia State House of Representatives from 1803 to 1807. He served as United States Senator from Georgia from 1813 to 1815, and was Secretary of War from 1815-16, and Secretary of the Treasury from 1816 to 1825. He then returned to Georgia and was elected a Circuit Judge.

SAMUEL DEXTER

Born: May 14, 1761. Died: May 4, 1816.

Dexter's portrait is on the third of three, 50¢ fourth issue notes.

At the early age of sixteen, he was admitted to Harvard College and graduated four years later in 1781. He became a Massachusetts Congressman from 1793 to 1795. He then became a Senator representing Massachusetts on March 4, 1799. In 1800, President John Adams asked Dexter to become the interim Secretary of War. He held this position for six months before becoming interim Secretary of the Treasury from January 1, 1801 until Thomas Jefferson's administration took over on March 4, 1801. He was unsuccessful in his run for Governor of Massachusetts in 1816, and died of scarlet fever just nine months later, on May 4, 1816.

WILLIAM PITT FESSENDEN

Born: October 16, 1806. Died: September 6, 1869.

His portrait is on the 25¢, third issue note.

Fessenden graduated college in 1823, studied law and passed the bar in 1827. He served in the House of Representatives from 1841-43, and as a Senator from 1854 to 1864. During the Civil War, Mr. Fessenden was Chairman of the Senate Committee on Finance. He proved very valuable to President Lincoln and Secretary Chase in helping to provide funds for the Union during time of war. In July, 1864, he succeeded Chase as Secretary of the Treasury. He was again elected as a Senator in 1865, and concluded his political career by casting the deciding vote against the impeachment of President Johnson.

GENERAL ULYSSES SIMPSON GRANT

Born: April 27, 1822. Died: July 23, 1885.

General Grant's portrait, along with General Sherman's is on the front of the 15¢, third issue, "Proof Only" notes.

He was appointed to West Point in 1839 and graduated in1843. He served in the Mexican War from 1845 to 1847. When the Civil War started, he was commissioned a Colonel in the Illinois 21st. Regiment. One of his first victories was on February 16, 1862, with the taking of Fort Donelson, Tennessee. He became known for the quote: "No terms except immediate and unconditional surrender."

Another important victory for Grant was on April 7, 1862 at Shiloh. On March 9, 1864, he was commissioned Lieutenant General by President Lincoln, and became General-in-Chief of all U.S. Armies. On April 9, 1865, General Lee surrendered to Grant at Appomattox Court House, Virginia. As we all know, General Grant went on to become President of the United States from March 4, 1869 to March 4, 1877.

THOMAS JEFFERSON

Born: April 13, 1743. Died: July 4, 1826.

Jefferson's portrait is on 5¢ and 25¢, first issue notes.

Thomas Jefferson graduated from William and Mary College in 1762. He was admitted to the bar in 1767. Jefferson was a member of the Virginia House from 1769-74. From 1775-76, he was a member of the Continental Congress. He drafted the Declaration of Independence and presented it to the Congress on July 2, 1776. Jefferson was Governor of Virginia from 1779-81 and was one of the first to report the discovery of gold in the United States, after finding a "lump" of gold by the side of the Rappahannock River in Virginia.

Jefferson was the first U.S. Minister to France from 1785-89, and was Secretary of State from 1790-93. In 1797, he became Vice-President of the United States and went on to become President from 1801-09. During his Presidency he spearheaded the Louisiana Purchase, doubling the size of the United States. In his retirement, he was one of the founders of the University of Virginia.

ABRAHAM LINCOLN

Born: February 12, 1809. Died: April 15, 1864.

Lincoln is on 50¢, fourth issue notes.

Interestingly enough, Lincoln's first office for the Federal Government was that of Postmaster, May, 1833, in New Salem, Illinois. A year before, when the Black Hawk Indian War started, Lincoln volunteered and was elected Captain of the 4th Illinois Company. The Oath of Allegiance is said to have been administered by Lieutenant Jefferson Davis to Captain Abraham Lincoln, twenty-eight years before they would be opposing presidents in the Civil War.

WILLIAM MORRIS MEREDITH

Born: June 8, 1799. Died: August 17, 1873.

William Meredith's portrait appears on the 10¢ fifth issue note.

Meredith was very intelligent, graduating from the University of Pennsylvania at only thirteen years of age. He was admitted to the bar by the time he was eighteen. President Taylor appointed him Secretary of the Treasury in 1849 and he served there until July, 1850.

GENERAL WILLIAM TECUMSEH SHERMAN

Born: February 8, 1820. Died: February 14, 1891.

General Sherman's portrait, along with General Grant's, appears on the 15¢, third issue specimen only notes.

Sherman was appointed to West Point in 1836, and graduated in 1840. He first saw service in the Florida Seminole Indian War as a lieutenant. He next saw action in the Mexican War from 1846-48. He served as the Superintendent of Louisana State University until it was closed because of the Civil War when he returned to military service. After the Union victory at Shiloh, April 7, 1862, he was promoted to Major General. Sherman is most remembered for his "March to the Sea". With some 98,000 troops, he captured Atlanta on September 1, 1864. Then went on to capture Savannah on December 23, 1864, where he sent a message to Lincoln, saying that this was a Christmas present from him. This victory split the South in half, speeding up the end of the war.

After the war, when Grant became President, he was promoted to Full General and given command of the United States Army. He retired in 1883 and is buried in Calvary Cemetery, St. Louis, MO.

FRANCIS ELLIS SPINNER

Born: January 21, 1802. Died: December 31, 1890.

General Spinner, known as the "Father of Fractional Currency" is depicted on the 50¢ third issue notes.

He began his business career as a cashier in erkimer, New York, and eventually became President of the Mohawk Valley Bank. He rose to Major-General in the state militia, and was elected to Congress for three consecutive terms, starting in 1854. After his Congressional term, President Lincoln appointed Spinner to be Treasurer of the United States. He served in this office from March 16, 1861 to June 30, 1875.

Spinner is described as the "Father of Postage and Fractional Currency" because he is responsible for the original design of small notes with the stamps pictured on them. He is also responsible for ordering the breakthrough technique of pasting 5¢ and 10¢ stamps to Treasury paper and demonstrating how it could be made more counterfeit proof by signing them. Spinner was instrumental in the success of the newly formed National Currency Bureau.

EDWIN STANTON

Born: December 19, 1814. Died: December 24, 1869.

Stanton was admitted to the bar in 1836. He served as a prosecuting attorney in Ohio from 1837 through 1839. In 1840 he moved his law practice to Pittsburgh, PA until moving to Washington, D.C. in 1856. President Buchanan named him Attorney General in 1860. Mr. Stanton became President Lincoln's Secretary of War in January 1862. President Johnson dismissed Stanton from his post in February, 1868. This culminated in the impeachment proceedings of President Johnson.

President Grant appointed Stanton to the Supreme Court in 1869 but Stanton died before he was able to take his seat on the court.

ROBERT JAMES WALKER

Born: July 23, 1801. Died: November 11, 1869.

Walker graduated from the University of Pennsylvania in 1819. He served in the U.S. Senate from 1838-45, and was Secretary of the Treasury from 1845-49. During the Civil War, he was the Financial Agent of the U.S. in Europe, where he sold over $200 million in U.S. Bonds to help pay for the war. While in Europe, he helped stop the sales of Confederate Bonds.

GEORGE WASHINGTON

Born: February 22, 1732. Died: December 12, 1799.

President Washington's portraits are on the following Postage and Fractional Currency notes: 10¢ and 50¢ First Issue; all the Second Issue notes (5¢, 10¢, 25¢ and 50¢); the 3¢ and 10¢ Third Issue notes; and the 25¢ Fourth Issue notes.

Most of us know something about George Washington, the father or our country. He was a county surveyor in Virginia in 1749. He was commissioned Lt. Colonel in 1754 when he helped to establish an outpost on the site that became the city of Pittsburgh of today. In 1755, he became Colonel, head of all Virginia troops, and married Martha Dandridge in 1759. Like Jefferson and Franklin, he was a 33° Freemason.

Washington was a member of the Virginia House of Burgesses from 1759 to 1774, and was a member of the Continental Congress, and in 1775, was elected to command all the Continental armies.

Washington became our first President on April 30, 1789,and was re-elected in 1793, but declined a third term in 1797. He retired to his farm in Virginia to raise tobacco and hemp.

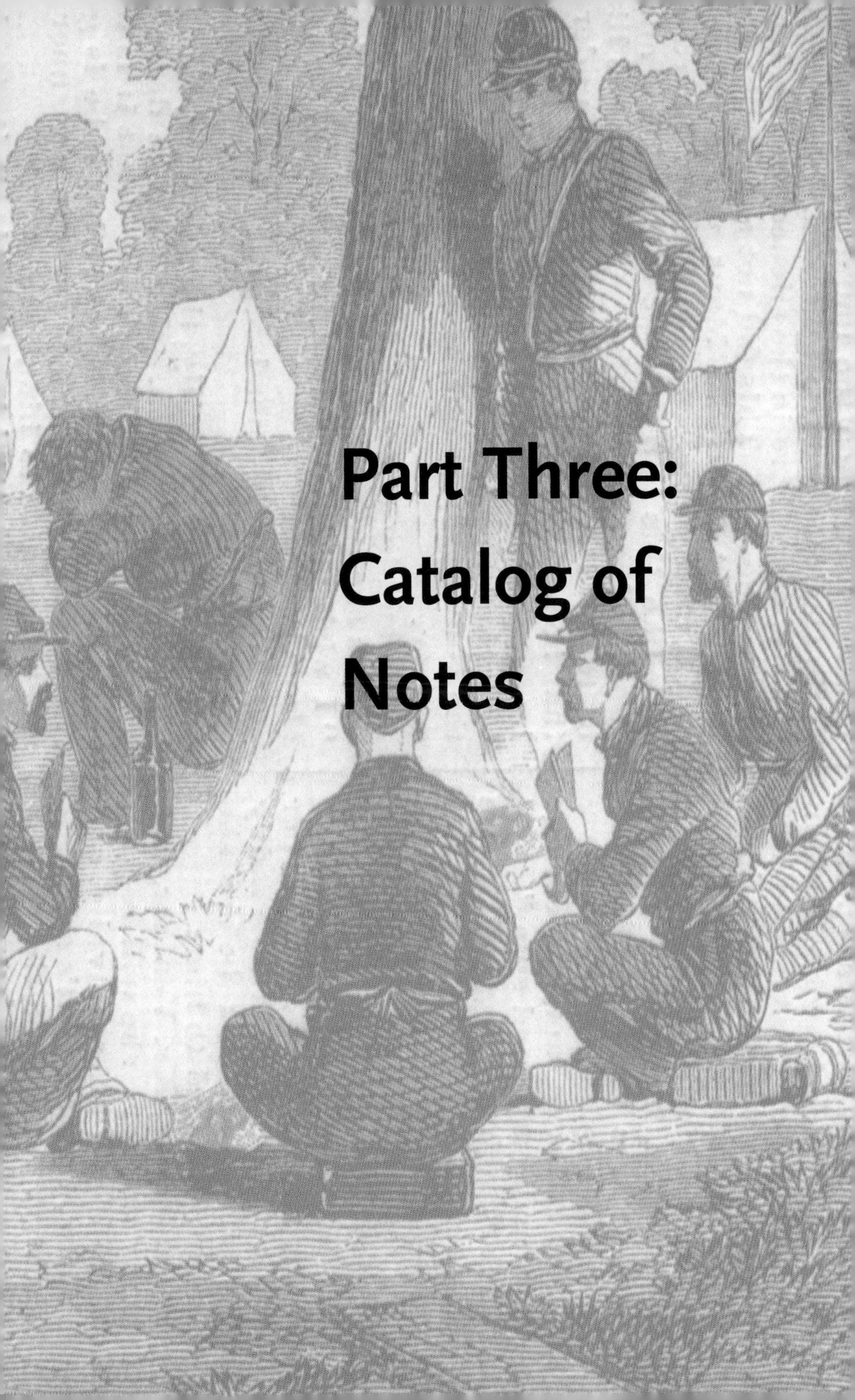

Part Three: Catalog of Notes

A Few Tips Before You Start Your Collection

1. Know your currency dealer. Trade with a dealer who has expertise and considerable experience in the currency market. Members of the "Professional Currency Dealers Association" are a good source.

(All members will display the PCDA logo in their advertising).

2. Share your collecting goals with your dealer. The more he or she knows, the better they can help you reach your goals.

3. Always buy the highest grade notes you can afford.

4. When choosing between notes of the same grade, select the one with the best "eye appeal".

5. Buying the higher grade (CHCU or GEM) notes is also a good investment. The higher grade notes are becoming very scarce because there is always a demand for high grade notes, but the supply is relatively fixed. The high grade notes are in constant demand by both collectors and dealers alike and you can almost always recover your investment and make a profit.

6. Enjoy the notes you buy. Show them off, but be sure to protect them in proper albums and with proper Mylar D®[1] or Melinex®[1] holders, obtainable from most reputable dealers, and full service coin shops.

They are made of Polyester Terephthalate which has no harsh chemicals. These holders offer excellent clarity and protection and the film that is used meets Library of Congress specifications for archival storage. Other types of holders have plasticizers that can break down and harm your notes.

Key to the Numbering System

Fr. # – The most widely used currency numbering system is known as the Friedberg System and was developed by Robert Friedberg.

MILT# – Numbering system for Postage and Fractional Currency developed by Milton R. Friedberg. The only system to number every different note of Postage and Fractional Currency. (See Guide which follows.)

1- Trademark of DuPont Teijin Films

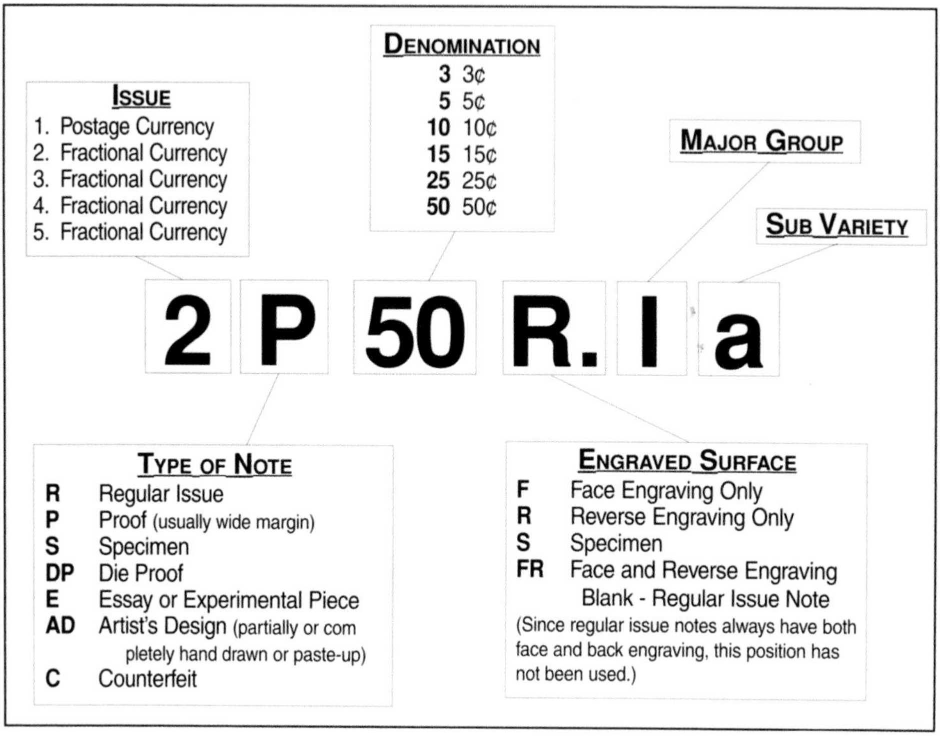

Above: Guide to the Milton Numbering System (MILT#). Reproduced from "The Encyclopedia of United States Fractional and Postal Currency", by Milton R. Friedberg, 1978

First Issue – Five Cent Postage Currency

Fr. 1228, Front

Fr. 1229, Back   *Fr. 1230, Back*

Perforated Edges with ABCO Monogram on Back

FR #	VG	VF	XF	AU	CU	CH-CU (63)	GEM (65)	S-GEM (66)	RARITY
1228	45	70	125	175	305	500	900	1200	SCARCE

Perforated Edges with No Monogram on Back

FR #	VG	VF	XF	AU	CU	CH-CU (63)	GEM (65)	S-GEM (66)	RARITY
1229	70	95	170	250	425	625	1100	1600	SCARCE

Straight Edges with ABCO Monogram on Back

FR #	VG	VF	XF	AU	CU	CH-CU (63)	GEM (65)	S-GEM (66)	RARITY
1230	30	45	50	65	125	300	500	650	VERY COMMON

Straight Edges with No Monogram on Back

FR #	VG	VF	XF	AU	CU	CH-CU (63)	GEM (65)	S-GEM (66)	RARITY
1231	50	75	125	200	395	550	895	1200	VERY SCARCE

SIZE

43-44 mm x 64-66 mm. Printed in sheets of 20 notes.

WHAT TO LOOK FOR

When buying a perforated note, take into consideration the quality of the perforations. A Gem note must have full perforations on all four sides. Also the perforations should not cut into the design of the note. In this series there are typically twelve perforations per 20 mm.

First Issue – Ten Cent Postage Currency

Fr. 1240, Front

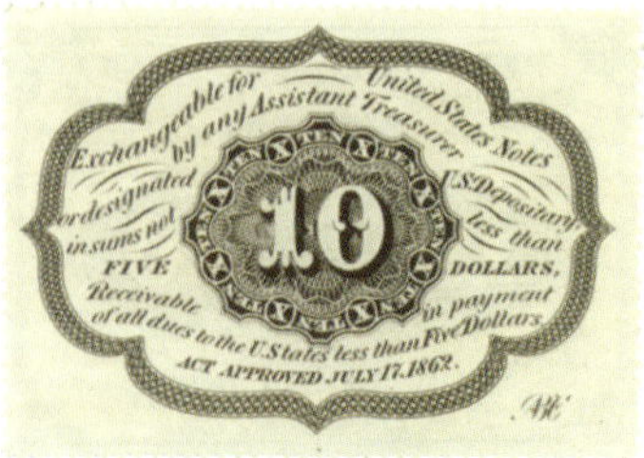

Fr. 1240, Back

Fr. 1243, Back

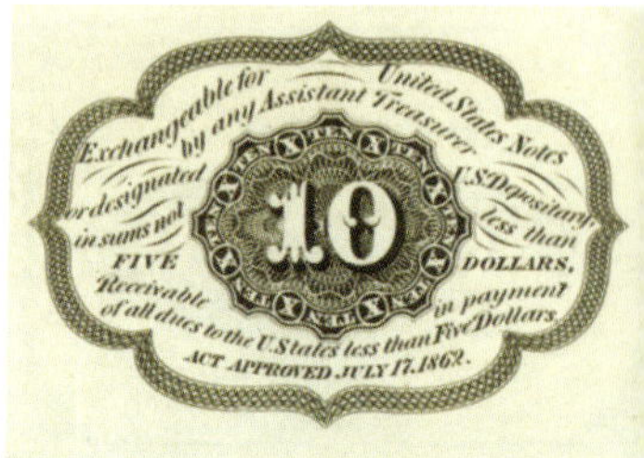

Perforated Edges with ABCO Monogram on Back

FR #	VG	VF	XF	AU	CU	CH-CU (63)	GEM (65)	S-GEM (66)	RARITY
1240	75	110	175	300	425	750	1000	1400	SCARCE

Perforated Edges with no Monogram on Back

FR #	VG	VF	XF	AU	CU	CH-CU (63)	GEM (65)	S-GEM (66)	RARITY
1241	80	125	200	300	450	950	1200	–	VERY SCARCE

Straight Edges with ABCO Monogram on Back

FR #	VG	VF	XF	AU	CU	CH-CU (63)	GEM (65)	S-GEM (66)	RARITY
1242	30	50	70	75	125	225	495	700	VERY COMMON

Straight Edges with no Monogram on Back

FR #	VG	VF	XF	AU	CU	CH-CU (63)	GEM (65)	S-GEM (66)	RARITY
1243	100	125	250	350	450	650	1400	–	VERY SCARCE

SIZE

43-44 mm x 64-66 mm. Printed in sheets of 20 notes.

WHAT TO LOOK FOR

When buying a perforated note, take into consideration the quality of the perforations. A Gem note must have full perforations on all four sides. Also the perforations should not cut into the design of the note. In this series there are typically twelve perforations per 20 mm.

First Issue –Twenty-five Cent Postage Currency

Fr. 1279, Front

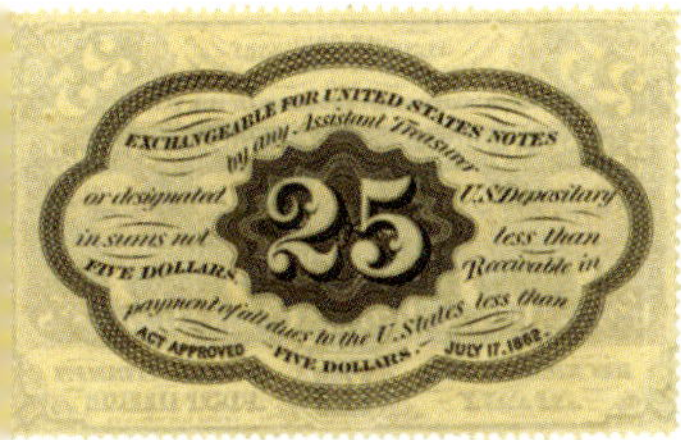

Fr. 1280, Back

Fr. 1281, Back

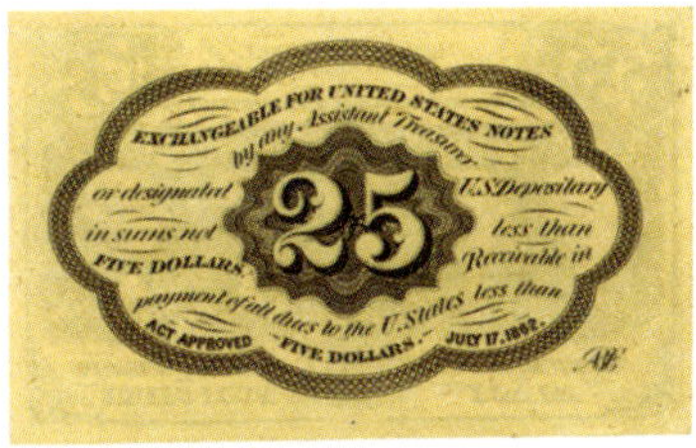

Perforated Edges with ABCO Monogram on Back

FR #	VG	VF	XF	AU	CU	CH-CU (63)	GEM (65)	S-GEM (66)	RARITY
1279	50	75	125	210	395	750	1200	–	SCARCE

Perforated Edges with no Monogram on Back

FR #	VG	VF	XF	AU	CU	CH-CU (63)	GEM (65)	S-GEM (66)	RARITY
1280	100	200	205	395	550	1000	1800	2300	VERY SCARCE

Straight Edges with ABCO Monogram on Back

FR #	VG	VF	XF	AU	CU	CH-CU (63)	GEM (65)	S-GEM (66)	RARITY
1281	30	50	70	110	200	310	550	–	COMMON

Straight Edges with no Monogram on Back

FR #	VG	VF	XF	AU	CU	CH-CU (63)	GEM (65)	S-GEM (66)	RARITY
1282	100	125	195	395	550	900	2000	–	VERY SCARCE

SIZE

64-67 mm x 44-46 mm. Printed in sheets of 16 notes.

WHAT TO LOOK FOR

Buy perforated notes, with full perforations on all four sides.

First Issue – Fifty Cent Postage Currency

Fr. 1310, Front

Fr. 1311, Back Fr. 1312, Back

Perforated Edges with ABCO Monogram on Back

FR #	VG	VF	XF	AU	CU	CH-CU (63)	GEM (65)	S-GEM (66)	RARITY
1310	75	110	300	500	695	900	1600	2500	SCARCE

Perforated Edges with no Monogram on Back

FR #	VG	VF	XF	AU	CU	CH-CU (63)	GEM (65)	S-GEM (66)	RARITY
1311	100	210	350	550	750	1000	1400	–	VERY SCARCE SLEEPER

Straight Edges with ABCO Monogram on Back

FR #	VG	VF	XF	AU	CU	CH-CU (63)	GEM (65)	S-GEM (66)	RARITY
1312	39	65	90	125	195	300	450	650	COMMON

Straight Edges with no Monogram on Back

FR #	VG	VF	XF	AU	CU	CH-CU (63)	GEM (65)	S-GEM (66)	RARITY
1313	145	250	395	595	900	1800	4500	–	VERY SCARCE SLEEPER RARE IN GEM

SIZE

64-67 mm x 44-46 mm. Printed in sheets of 16 notes.

WHAT TO LOOK FOR

On the Fr. 1311 and Fr. 1313, beware of removed ABCO monogram. Buy notes with full perforations on all four sides.

Second Issue – Five Cent Fractional Currency

Fr. 1232, Front

Fr. 1232, Back

Fr. 1233, Back

Fr. 1234, Back

Fr. 1235, Back

Without Surcharges on Corners on Back of Note

FR #	VG	VF	XF	AU	CU	CH-CU (63)	GEM (65)	S-GEM (66)	RARITY
1232	25	35	45	50	75	135	450	595	VERY COMMON

With Surcharges "18-63" on Bottom Corners on Back of Note

FR #	VG	VF	XF	AU	CU	CH-CU (63)	GEM (65)	S-GEM (66)	RARITY
1233	30	50	70	95	125	225	495	–	COMMON

With Surcharges "𝔖-18-63" on Corners on Back of Note

FR #	VG	VF	XF	AU	CU	CH-CU (63)	GEM (65)	S-GEM (66)	RARITY
1234	35	70	90	125	170	300	550	–	SCARCE

With Surcharges "ℜ-18-63" on Corners on Back of Note, Fiber Paper

FR #	VG	VF	XF	AU	CU	CH-CU (63)	GEM (65)	S-GEM (66)	RARITY
1235	75	200	300	575	825	1000	2000	–	VERY SCARCE RARE IN GEM

Second Issue –Five Cent Fractional Currency

SIZE

46-48 mm x 64-67 mm. Printed in sheets of 20 notes.

WHAT TO LOOK FOR

Most notes in this series are not well centered. The fiber paper note is almost always cut close at one end, often into the design. True Gems (those notes with good centering on both sides) are very hard to find. You must also take into account the surcharges on the back corners. A note cannot be a Gem unless the surcharges are clear and readable. Do not buy notes with blurred, unreadable surcharges, as they would be worth 20%-50% less. Also, try to buy notes with bright bronzing. In some cases the bronzing has turned green due to oxidation, resulting in a lower quality note.

Second Issue –Ten Cent Fractional Currency

Fr. 1244, Front

Fr. 1244, Back

Fr. 1245, Back

Fr. 1246, Back

Fr. 1247, Back

Without Surcharges on Corners on Back of Note

FR #	VG	VF	XF	AU	CU	CH-CU (63)	GEM (65)	S-GEM (66)	RARITY
1244	25	35	50	75	125	225	450	650	VERY COMMON

With Surcharges "18-63" on Bottom Corners on Back of Note

FR #	VG	VF	XF	AU	CU	CH-CU (63)	GEM (65)	S-GEM (66)	RARITY
1245	20	50	75	110	155	225	450	–	COMMON

With Surcharges "S-18-63" on Corners on Back of Note

FR #	VG	VF	XF	AU	CU	CH-CU (63)	GEM (65)	S-GEM (66)	RARITY
1246	32	65	100	125	250	390	795	–	SCARCE

With Surcharges "1-18-63" on Corners on Back of Note

FR #	VG	VF	XF	AU	CU	CH-CU (63)	GEM (65)	S-GEM (66)	RARITY
1247	75	110	175	250	325	500	895	1200	VERY SCARCE

Second Issue –Ten Cent Fractional Currency

Fr. 1248, Back

Fr. 1249, Back

With Surcharges “𝔒-18-63” on Corners on Back of Note

FR #	VG	VF	XF	AU	CU	CH-CU (63)	GEM (65)	S-GEM (66)	RARITY
1248	350	1000	1700	2300	2700	3600	5500	–	RARE LESS THAN 30 KNOWN

With Surcharges “𝔗-18-63” on Corners on Back of Note. Fiber Paper

FR #	VG	VF	XF	AU	CU	CH-CU (63)	GEM (65)	S-GEM (66)	RARITY
1249	100	175	350	450	650	900	2500	–	VERY SCARCE

SIZE

46-48 mm x 64-67 mm. Printed in sheets of 20 notes.

WHAT TO LOOK FOR

Special Note: With one exception, on all known Fr. 1248 notes the “O” and “63” surcharges are printed in a plain font style. Like all the other second issue notes, the one Fr. 1248 exception has the surcharges printed in an ornate, old roman style font “O“. This is the only genuine note, and, in my opinion, all of the others are forgeries.

Second Issue – Twenty-five Cent Fractional Currency

Fr. 1283, Back

Fr. 1283, Back

Fr. 1284, Back

Fr. 1285, Back

Fr. 1286, Back

Without Surcharges on Corners on Back of Note

FR #	VG	VF	XF	AU	CU	CH-CU (63)	GEM (65)	S-GEM (66)	RARITY
1283	30	50	79	125	225	290	495	695	COMMON

With Surcharges "18-63" on Bottom Corners on Back of Note

FR #	VG	VF	XF	AU	CU	CH-CU (63)	GEM (65)	S-GEM (66)	RARITY
1284	32	65	120	200	300	450	700	–	SCARCE

With Surcharges "𝔞-18-63" on Corners on Back of Note

FR #	VG	VF	XF	AU	CU	CH-CU (63)	GEM (65)	S-GEM (66)	RARITY
1285	35	69	100	150	225	325	595	–	SCARCE

With Surcharges "𝔰-18-63" on Corners on Back of Note

FR #	VG	VF	XF	AU	CU	CH-CU (63)	GEM (65)	S-GEM (66)	RARITY
1286	35	59	100	200	300	450	900	–	SCARCE

Second Issue – Twenty-five Cent Fractional Currency

Fr. 1288, Back

Fr. 1289, Back

Fr. 1290, Back

With Surcharges "Ⓣ-18-63" on Corners on Back of Note

FR #	VG	VF	XF	AU	CU	CH-CU (63)	GEM (65)	S-GEM (66)	RARITY
1288	75	110	150	250	395	500	1200	–	SCARCE+

With Surcharges "𝔗-1-18-63" on Corners on Back of Note, Fiber Paper

FR #	VG	VF	XF	AU	CU	CH-CU (63)	GEM (65)	S-GEM (66)	RARITY
1289	100	125	195	350	700	900	1800	–	VERY SCARCE+

With Surcharges "𝔗-2-18-63" on Corners on Back of Note, Fiber Paper

FR #	VG	VF	XF	AU	CU	CH-CU (63)	GEM (65)	S-GEM (66)	RARITY
1290	90	150	200	295	550	900	1800	–	VERY SCARCE

SIZE

46-48 mm x 64-67 mm. Printed in sheets of 20 notes.

WHAT TO LOOK FOR

The Fr. 1286A is a variety that comes with a slate colored back, with NO trace of violet or purple. These notes are worth three times the amount of the much more common Fr. 1286. There are less than thirty known. Most 1286 type notes are poorly centered. Fiber paper notes are almost always cut close on one end or the other. True Gems (those with good centering on both sides and clear surcharges) are very hard to find. Many notes have blurred surcharges. Buy notes with clear, readable surcharges and bright bronzing.

Second Issue – Fifty Cent Fractional Currency

Fr. 1316, Front

Fr. 1316, Back

Fr. 1317, Back

Fr. 1318, Back

Fr. 1320, Back

With Surcharges "18-63" on Corners on Back of Note

FR #	VG	VF	XF	AU	CU	CH-CU (63)	GEM (65)	S-GEM (66)	RARITY
1316	35	70	100	170	325	425	795	–	VERY SCARCE

With Surcharges "𝔞-18-63" on Corners on Back of Note

FR #	VG	VF	XF	AU	CU	CH-CU (63)	GEM (65)	S-GEM (66)	RARITY
1317	35	70	100	150	325	425	900	1200	SCARCE

With Surcharges "1-18-63" on Corners on Back of Note

FR #	VG	VF	XF	AU	CU	CH-CU (63)	GEM (65)	S-GEM (66)	RARITY
1318	50	75	125	210	350	500	950	1400	SCARCE

With Surcharges "𝔒-1-18-63" on Corners on Back of Note, Fiber Paper

FR #	VG	VF	XF	AU	CU	CH-CU (63)	GEM (65)	S-GEM (66)	RARITY
1320	75	110	200	295	450	650	1400	–	VERY SCARCE

There are no specimens known of Fr. 1314, described as without surcharges on corners of back of note.

No. 1319 does not exist. What was once thought to be a "𝔖-2-18-63" surcharge is in reality a "𝔗."

Second Issue – Fifty Cent Fractional Currency

Fr. 1321 Back

Fr. 1322 Back

With Surcharges "R-2-18-63" on Corners on Back of Note, Fiber Paper

FR #	VG	VF	XF	AU	CU	CH-CU (63)	GEM (65)	S-GEM (66)	RARITY
1321	90	200	450	700	900	1200	2000	–	VERY SCARCE RARE IN GEM

With Surcharges "T-1-18-63" on Corners on Back of Note, Fiber Paper

FR #	VG	VF	XF	AU	CU	CH-CU (63)	GEM (65)	S-GEM (66)	RARITY
1322	75	110	175	295	450	650	1295	–	SCARCE

SIZE

45-48.5 mm x 63-66.25 mm. Printed in sheets of 20 notes.

WHAT TO LOOK FOR

Fiber paper notes are almost always cut close on one end or the other. True Gems (those with good centering on both sides and clear surcharges) are very hard to find. Many notes have blurred surcharges. Buy notes with clear, readable surcharges and bright bronzing.

Third Issue – Three Cent Fractional Currency

Fr. 1226, Back.

Fr. 1226, Front

Fr. 1227, Front

With Light Background to Portrait

FR #	VG	VF	XF	AU	CU	CH-CU (63)	GEM (65)	S-GEM (66)	RARITY
1226	35	50	95	100	145	260	550	750	COMMON

With Dark Background to Portrait

FR #	VG	VF	XF	AU	CU	CH-CU (63)	GEM (65)	S-GEM (66)	RARITY
1227	70	100	145	195	295	410	750	1200	SCARCE VERY SCARCE IN GEM

SIZE

39-42 mm x 64-68 mm. Printed in sheets of 25 notes.

WHAT TO LOOK FOR

Make sure there are good margins on all four sides, both front and back.

Third Issue – Five Cent Fractional Currency

Fr. 1236, Front

Fr. 1236, Back

Fr. 1238, Back

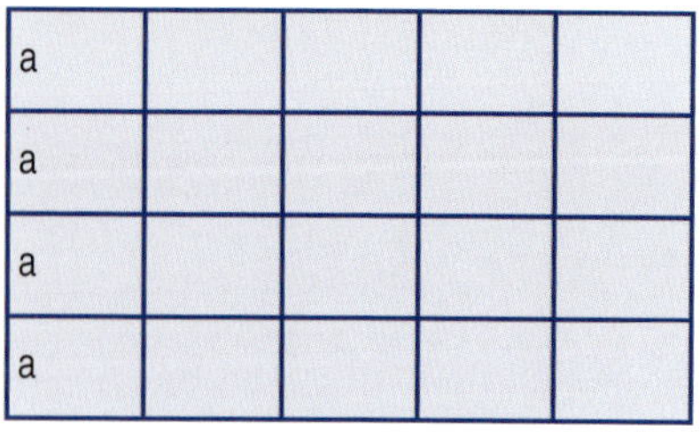

Location of sheet position of letter "a".
The "a" can be 1 mm to 1.4 mm in size.

Sheet Position Indicator

Red Back

FR #	VG	VF	XF	AU	CU	CH-CU (63)	GEM (65)	S-GEM (66)	RARITY
1236	30	50	110	195	295	450	700	–	SCARCE

Red Back with Sheet Position Indicator "a"

FR #	VG	VF	XF	AU	CU	CH-CU (63)	GEM (65)	S-GEM (66)	RARITY
1237	35	70	135	250	500	795	1400	–	VERY SCARCE

Green Back

FR #	VG	VF	XF	AU	CU	CH-CU (63)	GEM (65)	S-GEM (66)	RARITY
1238	25	45	90	100	155	200	450	–	VERY COMMON

Green Back with Sheet Position Indicator "a"

FR #	VG	VF	XF	AU	CU	CH-CU (63)	GEM (65)	S-GEM (66)	RARITY
1239	35	70	95	125	175	325	650	–	COMMON

Third Issue – Five Cent Fractional Currency

THE SPENCER MORTON CLARK NOTES

Spencer M. Clark, a civil service engineer, was appointed to the position of Chief Clerk at the National Currency Bureau (the predecessor to today's Bureau of Engraving & Printing). At the time the Bureau was located in the Treasury Department. He was a man of many talents: superb inventor, tireless organizer, and also a very competent administrator.

Clark made one BIG mistake, of putting his own portrait on the new, five cent third issue notes of Fractional Currency. This five cent note has the distinction of being the only note whose design forced Congress to pass a major piece of legislation. The outraged Congress promptly passed the law of April 7th, 1866, forbidding portrayal of a living person on any U.S. notes or bonds!

Then you say, how about the Fessenden 25¢ and Spinner 50¢ notes? Both were issued before April 7th 1866. Fessenden notes started in February, 1865 and the Spinner notes started in January 1866. In Section 12 the law said in part "if the plates had already been prepared, then the notes could be issued." The Grant/Sherman notes were not issued since their plates were not yet completed.

The decision was also made to abolish the five cent denomination of Fractional Currency. Shortly thereafter the Act of May 17th, 1866 directed that the nickel five cent piece be issued in quantities sufficient to redeem the outstanding five cent notes. As of June 1884 10.5 million had been redeemed, which still left over 2.5 million still outstanding.

From January 1865 to early April 1866 some 13,140,055 notes with Clark's portrait had been issued. For the first time, plate position identification was also used. On each 16-subject sheet (four rows, four columns) the column of notes at the far left shows a small letter "a" on each of those four notes. It's located on the left side of the note just below the midway down the note. Therefore the notes with the "a" position indicator are three times more scarce than the other twelve notes without the position indicator.

There are four varieties:

- Fr. 1236 - Red Back without the position indicator
- Fr. 1237 - Red Back with the "a" position indicator
- Fr. 1238 - Green Back without the position indicator
- Fr. 1239 - Green Back with the "a"

The red backs are much more scarce than the green backs. The Fr. 1236 notes are hard to find UNC or better and are rarely well-centered on both sides. The Fr. 1237 and the Fr. 1239 are hard to

Third Issue – Five Cent Fractional Currency

find without ink smears, since they were the notes at the left edge of the sheet. The Fr. 1237 are very hard to find UNC. or better. They often come with ink smears because they come from the left end of the sheet. The Fr. 1238 is the most common and can be found easily in UNC or better, while the Fr. 1239 is hard to find nice because of the ink smears as well.

SIZE

46 mm x 64 mm. Printed in sheets of 20 notes.

WHAT TO LOOK FOR

The Fr. 1236 notes are very hard to find and are rarely well centered on both sides. Fr. 1237 notes are often smeared because they came from the end of a sheet. (See Illustration). Ink smears are also common on the Fr. 1239 notes. In addition to frequent smears, the Fr. 1237 and Fr. 1239 were poorly printed on the left side due to less pressure on the plate towards the outer edges.

Third Issue – Ten Cent Fractional Currency

Fr. 1251, Front

Fr. 1251, Back

Fr. 1253, Front

Fr. 1254, Front

Fr. 1255, Back

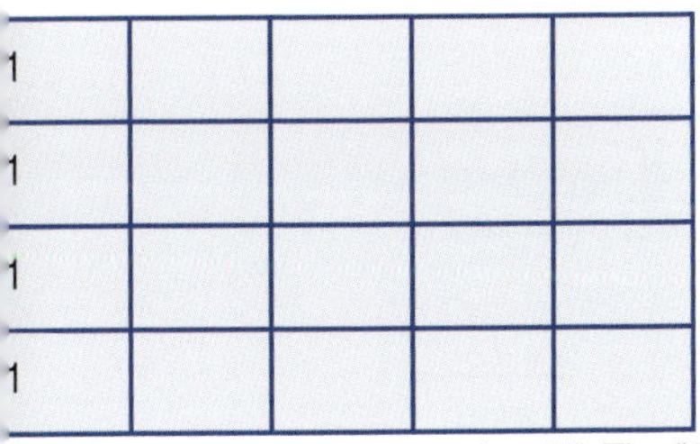

ocation of sheet position number "1". The "1" an be 1 mm to 1.4 mm in size.

Sheet Position Indicator

Red Back with Printed Signatures of Colby and Spinner

FR #	VG	VF	XF	AU	CU	CH-CU (63)	GEM (65)	S-GEM (66)	RARITY
1251	35	65	100	125	250	395	700	–	SCARCE

Red Back with Position Indicator "1" and Printed Signatures

FR #	VG	VF	XF	AU	CU	CH-CU (63)	GEM (65)	S-GEM (66)	RARITY
1252	45	70	125	200	395	550	1200	–	VERY SCARCE SLEEPER

Red Back with Autographed Signatures of Colby and Spinner

FR #	VG	VF	XF	AU	CU	CH-CU (63)	GEM (65)	S-GEM (66)	RARITY
1253	90	120	175	200	300	550	900	–	SCARCE

Third Issue – Ten Cent Fractional Currency

Red Back with Autographed Signatures of Jeffries and Spinner

FR #	VG	VF	XF	AU	CU	CH-CU (63)	GEM (65)	S-GEM (66)	RARITY
1254	100	125	200	275	450	650	1000	–	VERY SCARCE SLEEPER

Green Back with Printed Signatures of Colby and Spinner

FR #	VG	VF	XF	AU	CU	CH-CU (63)	GEM (65)	S-GEM (66)	RARITY
1255	25	45	50	65	100	139	500	700	COMMON

Green Back with Position Indicator "1" and Printed Signatures

FR #	VG	VF	XF	AU	CU	CH-CU (63)	GEM (65)	S-GEM (66)	RARITY
1256	39	55	75	100	195	325	550	750	COMMON

SIZE

46-48 mm x 80-82 mm. Printed in sheets of 16 notes.

WHAT TO LOOK FOR

I get many calls from people who think that they have a very rare Fr. 1255a, Colby and Spinner, Green Back, with autographed signatures. Check this fact before you call an appraiser. On a note with an autographed signature, the ink will not always be the same color throughout the signature. Ink usually bleeds through to the reverse. Ink will usually be darker where the letters intersect. A printed signature will always be the same color (usually black) throughout the signature. For autographed signatures, you should be able to see the signatures from the back of the note. There are only two known Fr. 1255a, neither of which will be offered for sale any time soon. The last public sale of one was the Tom O'Mara sale in St. Louis on May 5, 2005 where it sold for $138,000.

The Fr. 1252 and Fr. 1254 are, what I call, "sleeper" notes. These are increasing in value and are very hard to find in CHCU and Gem condition.

Third Issue – Twenty-five Cent Fractional Currency

Fr. 1291, Front

Fr. 1292, Back

Fr. 1292, Fr. 1295, Fr. 1298 & Fr. 1300 Sheet Position Indicator

Fr. 1294, Back

Red Back

FR #	VG	VF	XF	AU	CU	CH-CU (63)	GEM (65)	S-GEM (66)	RARITY
1291	50	75	120	225	300	595	900	1200	SCARCE

Red Back with Position Indicator “a” on the front

FR #	VG	VF	XF	AU	CU	CH-CU (63)	GEM (65)	S-GEM (66)	RARITY
1292	70	90	155	250	350	900	1100	1400	VERY SCARCE

Green Back

FR #	VG	VF	XF	AU	CU	CH-CU (63)	GEM (65)	S-GEM (66)	RARITY
1294	30	50	70	90	120	200	500	700	COMMON

Green Back with Position Indicator “a” on the front

FR #	VG	VF	XF	AU	CU	CH-CU (63)	GEM (65)	S-GEM (66)	RARITY
1295	35	70	100	115	200	350	595	900	COMMON

Third Issue – Twenty-five Cent Fractional Currency

Fr. 1297, Back

Fr.1296 Sheet Position Indicator: This is the rare variety with the extremely large "a" 7mm to the lower right of its normal position. The "a" is 2mm in size.

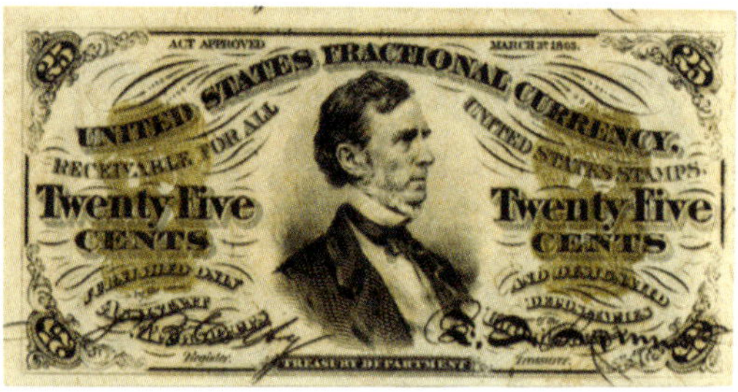

Fr. 1299, Front with Solid Surcharges

Location of sheet position letter "a". The "a" can be 0.9 mm to 1.2 mm in size.

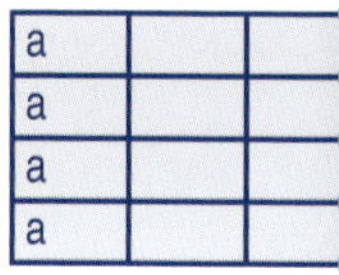

Green Back with Large Position Indicator "a" 7mm to the Lower Right than Normal

FR #	VG	VF	XF	AU	CU	CH-CU (63)	GEM (65)	S-GEM (66)	RARITY
1296	700	1400	2000	2900	4300	6500	9000	11000	VERY RARE

Green Back with Surcharges "m-2-6-5", Fiber Paper

FR #	VG	VF	XF	AU	CU	CH-CU (63)	GEM (65)	S-GEM (66)	RARITY
1297	45	75	125	300	450	650	1200	–	VERY SCARCE

Green Back with Surcharges "m-2-6-5", Fiber Paper, with position indicator "a"

FR #	VG	VF	XF	AU	CU	CH-CU (63)	GEM (65)	S-GEM (66)	RARITY
1298	55	100	225	450	700	900	2000	2700	EXTREMELY SCARCE

Green Back with Surcharges "m-2-6-5", Fiber Paper and Solid Front Bronze Surcharges

FR #	VG	VF	XF	AU	CU	CH-CU (63)	GEM (65)	S-GEM (66)	RARITY
1299	450	900	1400	1995	2100	3000	4300	–	RARE LESS THAN 30 KNOWN

Green Back with Surcharges "m-2-6-5", Fiber Paper, Position Indicator "a" and Solid Front Bronze Surcharges

FR #	VG	VF	XF	AU	CU	CH-CU (63)	GEM (65)	S-GEM (66)	RARITY
1300	900	2000	4100	4800	5900	7000	–	–	VERY RARE LESS THAN 20 KNOWN

3rd ISSUE BACK SURCHARGES

The twenty-five cent Fessenden notes Fr. 1297, Fr. 1299, Fr. 1299 and Fr. 1300 were printed March 22nd, 1865. They were printed on fiber paper, sometimes called membrane or spider leg paper. The paper was made up of two sheets of thin paper with the membranes, or spider legs, sandwiched between the sheets. The back surcharges therefore make sense! The back surcharge M-2-6-5, "M" for membrane paper, "2" for two sheets of paper, and "6-5" for when they were printed – 1865.

SIZE

46-48 mm x 94-97 mm. Printed in sheets of 12 notes.

WHAT TO LOOK FOR

The fiber paper notes listed as Fr. 1297 - Fr. 1300 are thick, coarse fiber paper, not the thin fiber paper of the second issue notes. These fiber notes can also be brittle, so beware of corners chipping off and other damage.

Third Issue – Fifty Cent Fractional Currency: Justice

Fr. 1343, Front

"1" Sheet Position Indicator

"a" Sheet Position Indicator

Fr. 1343, Front

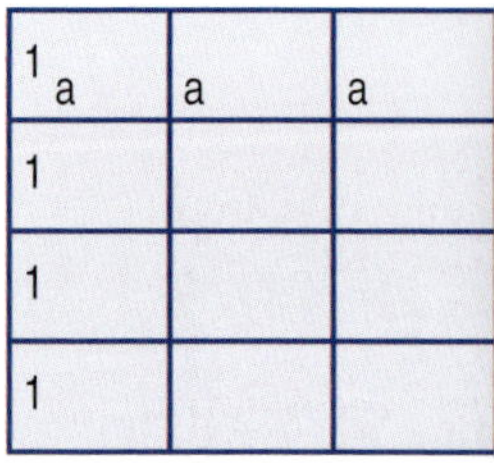

Sheet position indicator location.
Size of the "1" can be 0.8 mm to 2.25 mm.
Size of the "a" can be 0.8 mm to 2 mm.

Red Back without Surcharges, without Position Indicator

FR #	VG	VF	XF	AU	CU	CH-CU (63)	GEM (65)	S-GEM (66)	RARITY
1343	100	125	200	300	495	725	1000	1200	SCARCE

Red Back without Surcharges, with Position Indicator "1" and "a" on the Front

FR #	VG	VF	XF	AU	CU	CH-CU (63)	GEM (65)	S-GEM (66)	RARITY
1344	500	750	1600	3200	3500	5500	7000	–	RARE

Red Back without Surcharges, with Position Indicator "1" on the Front

FR #	VG	VF	XF	AU	CU	CH-CU (63)	GEM (65)	S-GEM (66)	RARITY
1345	100	125	200	350	500	695	1000	–	SCARCE

Red Back without Surcharges, with Position Indicator "a" on the Front

FR #	VG	VF	XF	AU	CU	CH-CU (63)	GEM (65)	S-GEM (66)	RARITY
1346	100	125	200	395	525	700	1000	–	VERY SCARCE

Third Issue – Fifty Cent Fractional Currency: Justice

Fr. 1347, Back

Fr. 1351, Back

Red Back with Surcharge "𝔞-2-6-5" without Position Indicator

FR #	VG	VF	XF	AU	CU	CH-CU (63)	GEM (65)	S-GEM (66)	RARITY
1347	100	125	200	395	525	700	1000	--	SCARCE

Red Back with Surcharge "𝔞-2-6-5" with Position Indicator "1" and "a" on the Front

FR #	VG	VF	XF	AU	CU	CH-CU (63)	GEM (65)	S-GEM (66)	RARITY
1348	600	1200	1800	2300	3000	4500	7900		RARE

Red Back with Surcharge "𝔞-2-6-5" with Position Indicator "1" on the Front

FR #	VG	VF	XF	AU	CU	CH-CU (63)	GEM (65)	S-GEM (66)	RARITY
1349	100	210	350	495	595	795	1295	–	VERY SCARCE

Red Back with Surcharge "𝔞-2-6-5" with Position Indicator "a" on the Front

FR #	VG	VF	XF	AU	CU	CH-CU (63)	GEM (65)	S-GEM (66)	RARITY
1350	135	250	425	595	795	1000	1600	–	RARE

Red Back, Surcharge "𝔰-2-6-4", Printed Signatures, Fiber Paper, No Position Indicators

FR #	VG	VF	XF	AU	CU	CH-CU (63)	GEM (65)	S-GEM (66)	RARITY
1351	–	7000	10000	14000	19000	30000	46000	–	VERY RARE

Red Back, Surcharge "𝔰-2-6-4", Printed Signatures, Fiber Paper, "1" and "a" Position Indicators

FR #	VG	VF	XF	AU	CU	CH-CU (63)	GEM (65)	S-GEM (66)	RARITY
1352	–	50000	70000	–	–	–	125-130K	–	*

Only three known

Third Issue – Fifty Cent Fractional Currency: Justice

Fr. 1355, Front

Fr. 1358, Back

Red Back, Surcharge “𝔖-2-6-4”, Printed Signatures, Fiber Paper, “1” Position Indicato

FR #	VG	VF	XF	AU	CU	CH-CU (63)	GEM (65)	S-GEM (66)	RARITY
1353		9000	12900	15000	21000	25000	–	–	VERY RARE

Red Back, Surcharge “𝔖-2-6-4”, Printed Signatures, Fiber Paper, “a” Position Indicato

FR #	VG	VF	XF	AU	CU	CH-CU (63)	GEM (65)	S-GEM (66)	RARITY
1354		11000	16000	20000	23000	29000	–	–	VERY RARE

Red Back without Surcharges, Autographed Signatures without Position Indicators

FR #	VG	VF	XF	AU	CU	CH-CU (63)	GEM (65)	S-GEM (66)	RARITY
1355	110	175	250	350	495	595	1200	–	SCARCE

Red Back, Surcharges “𝔄-2-6-5”, Autographed Signatures without Position Indicators

FR #	VG	VF	XF	AU	CU	CH-CU (63)	GEM (65)	S-GEM (66)	RARITY
1356	125	225	325	495	595	750	1400	–	VERY SCARCE

Red Back, Surcharges “𝔖-2-6-4”, Autographed Signatures, Fiber Paper

FR #	VG	VF	XF	AU	CU	CH-CU (63)	GEM (65)	S-GEM (66)	RARITY
1357	200	575	825	1400	2000	3200	9000	–	**

Green Back without Surcharges, without Position Indicator

FR #	VG	VF	XF	AU	CU	CH-CU (63)	GEM (65)	S-GEM (66)	RARITY
1358	100	120	195	300	450	750	1500	–	SCARCE

** *Very Scarce. Becomes Rare in CU to ChCU and Very Rare in Gem*

Third Issue – Fifty Cent Fractional Currency: Justice

Fr. 1362, Back. Compactly Spaced Surcharges.

Fr. 1367, Back. Widely Spaced Surcharges.

Green Back without Surcharges, with Position Indicator "1" and "a" on the Front

FR #	VG	VF	XF	AU	CU	CH-CU (63)	GEM (65)	S-GEM (66)	RARITY
1359	450	900	1400	1800	2300	3700	5000	–	RARE

Green Back without Surcharges, with Position Indicator "1" on the Front

FR #	VG	VF	XF	AU	CU	CH-CU (63)	GEM (65)	S-GEM (66)	RARITY
1360	78	100	200	350	495	750	1400	–	VERY SCARCE

Green Back without Surcharges, with Position Indicator "a" on the Front

FR #	VG	VF	XF	AU	CU	CH-CU (63)	GEM (65)	S-GEM (66)	RARITY
1361	100	125	225	375	550	875	1200	–	SOMEWHAT RARE

Green Back with Surcharge "a-2-6-5" Compactly Spaced 92mm X 30mm, without Position Indicator

FR #	VG	VF	XF	AU	CU	CH-CU (63)	GEM (65)	S-GEM (66)	RARITY
1362	100	125	225	325	475	595	900	–	COMMON

Green Back with Surcharge "a-2-6-5" Compactly Spaced 92mm X 30mm, with Position Indicators "1" and "a"

FR #	VG	VF	XF	AU	CU	CH-CU (63)	GEM (65)	S-GEM (66)	RARITY
1363	135	275	425	625	825	1000	1400	–	VERY SCARCE

Green Back with Surcharge "a-2-6-5" Compactly Spaced 92mm X 30mm, with Position Indicator "1"

FR #	VG	VF	XF	AU	CU	CH-CU (63)	GEM (65)	S-GEM (66)	RARITY
1364	100	115	175	350	595	750	995	–	SCARCE

Green Back with Surcharge "a-2-6-5" Compactly Spaced 92mm X 30mm, with Position Indicator "a"

FR #	VG	VF	XF	AU	CU	CH-CU (63)	GEM (65)	S-GEM (66)	RARITY
1365	100	125	200	325	495	795	1000	–	SCARCE

Third Issue – Fifty Cent Fractional Currency: Justice

Fr. 1373A, Back

Green Back with Surcharge “𝔞-2-6-5” Widely Spaced 98mm X 34mm, without Position Indicator

FR #	VG	VF	XF	AU	CU	CH-CU (63)	GEM (65)	S-GEM (66)	RARITY
1366	100	200	300	395	550	825	1200	–	VERY SCARCE

Green Back with Surcharge “𝔞-2-6-5” Widely Spaced 98mm X 34mm, with Position Indicators “1” and “a

FR #	VG	VF	XF	AU	CU	CH-CU (63)	GEM (65)	S-GEM (66)	RARITY
1367	750	1600	2000	3000	5000	9000	–	–	VERY RARE SLEEPER

Green Back with Surcharge “𝔞-2-6-5” Widely Spaced 98mm X 34mm, with Position Indicator “1”

FR #	VG	VF	XF	AU	CU	CH-CU (63)	GEM (65)	S-GEM (66)	RARITY
1368	200	450	525	700	900	2000	3500	–	RARE

Green Back with Surcharge “𝔞-2-6-5” Widely Spaced 98mm X 34mm,with Position Indicator “a”

FR #	VG	VF	XF	AU	CU	CH-CU (63)	GEM (65)	S-GEM (66)	RARITY
1369	250	525	650	795	900	1600	2500	–	RARE

Green Back with Surcharge “𝔞-2-6-5”, without Position Indicator, Fiber Paper

FR #	VG	VF	XF	AU	CU	CH-CU (63)	GEM (65)	S-GEM (66)	RARITY
1370	155	300	375	500	895	1200	1900	–	VERY SCARCE

Green Back with Surcharge “𝔞-2-6-5” with Position Indicators “1” and “a”, Fiber Paper

FR #	VG	VF	XF	AU	CU	CH-CU (63)	GEM (65)	S-GEM (66)	RARITY
1371		1600	2000	3000	4500	5900	19000	–	VERY RARE SLEEPER

Green Back with Surcharge “𝔞-2-6-5” with Position Indicator “1”, Fiber Paper

FR #	VG	VF	XF	AU	CU	CH-CU (63)	GEM (65)	S-GEM (66)	RARITY
1372		350	450	795	1000	1600	2500	–	RARE

Green Back with Surcharge “𝔞-2-6-5” with Position Indicator “a”, Fiber Paper

FR #	VG	VF	XF	AU	CU	CH-CU (63)	GEM (65)	S-GEM (66)	RARITY
1373		370	450	795	1000	1600	3000	–	RARE

Green Back with Surcharge “𝔰-2-6-4” without Position Indicators, Fiber Paper

FR #	VG	VF	XF	AU	CU	CH-CU (63)	GEM (65)	S-GEM (66)	RARITY
1373A	–	–	–	46000	–	–	–	–	*

* *Only Nine known. Two pairs and five singles. Very rare. The highest price paid for an individual note was $46,000 in AU condition.*

Third Issue – Fifty Cent Fractional Currency: Justice

3rd ISSUE BACK SURCHARGES

The first Justice notes to be printed – Fr. 1351, Fr. 1352, Fr. 1353, Fr. 1354, Fr. 1357 and Fr. 1373a – were printed December 5th, 1864. The fibers are smaller in size than those of the twenty-five cent Fessenden notes, more like spider legs, which indicates that the Justice notes are on a different type of fiber paper. The back surcharge "𝔖-2-6-4", also makes sense; the "𝔖" for spider legs paper, "2" for two sheets of paper and "6-4" for the year they were printed, 1864. All these notes were printed with red backs except the Fr. 1373a, the only green back note with the "𝔖-2-6-4" surcharge.

The Fr. 1370 through Fr. 1373 were also fiber paper notes. These notes, bearing the "A-2-6-5" surcharge on the back, were produced in 1865.

SIZE

46-50 mm x 113-115 mm. Printed in sheets of 12 notes.

WHAT TO LOOK FOR

Fr. 1343 Can be found in GEM. Justice notes only need 1mm margins on the front on all four sides to make GEM status due to sheet layout being tight. GEM backs need to be well centered.

Fr. 1344 Many of these notes come with a preprinted wrinkle near the top center. This does not affect the grades. There are less than twenty five known. Perhaps five of these are GEMS.

Fr. 1345 Can be found in GEM.

Fr. 1346 Can be found in GEM.

Fr. 1347 Can be found in GEM. Check the back centering. They are sometimes cut close to the left.

Fr. 1348 There are less than twenty known.

Fr. 1349 Should have good embossing. Can be found in GEM.

Fr. 1350 Can be found in GEM. Besides good centering on both sides, they should be good color, bright bronzing and good, deep embossing.

Fr. 1351 There are twelve to fifteen known.

Fr. 1352 There are only three known.

Fr. 1353 There are only eight or nine known.

Fr. 1354 There are only seven or eight known.

Fr. 1355 Most common autographed Justice note. GEMs can be found, but most are CHCU. On all autographed notes, make sure there are no ink "burn holes".

Third Issue – Fifty Cent Fractional Currency: Justice

Fr. 1356 Can be found in GEM.

Fr. 1357 If you are collecting GEMs, don't wait for this one. But that real nice CHCU with good embossing and bright bronzing. There is only one GEM known, and there are only twenty three to twenty five uncirculated or CHCUs known.

Fr. 1358 Can be found in GEM. Should come with bright bronzing and good embossing.

Fr. 1359 Again, buy that nice CHCU. No GEMs are known. Most are cut close or into the design on the left and/or the bottom. There are only twenty or so known.

Fr. 1360 Can be found in GEM.

Fr. 1361 Very hard to fine in GEM.

Fr. 1362 Can be found in GEM. This is the most common of the Justice notes.

Fr. 1363 Can be found in GEM. Should come with good embossing and bright bronzing.

Fr. 1364 Can be found in GEM. Should come with good embossing.

Fr. 1365 Very tough, but can be found in GEM.

Fr. 1366 Can be found in GEM.

Fr. 1367 There are less than fifteen known. Very hard to find uncirculated or better. An undervalued note.

Fr. 1368 Very few GEMs known. Another undervalued note that is very tough to find in any grade.

Fr. 1369 Very difficult to find in any grade, with very few GEMs known.

Fr. 1370 Only a few GEMs known. Fiber paper GEMs are all rare.

Fr. 1371 There are less than twenty known. Very hard to find uncirculated or better. With maybe only five to seven CHCUs, this is an undervalued note.

Fr. 1372 Very few GEMs. CHCU come with good embossing.

Fr. 1373 Also very few GEMs known. Should also have good embossing.

Fr. 1373A Only nine known. There was a block of eight in the 1903 Friedman collection. It was creased twice through the notes. Therefore, all eight are, at best AU.

Third Issue – Fifty Cent Fractional Currency: Spinner

Fr. 1324, Front

Fr. 1324, Back

Fr. 1328, Front

Red Back with Surcharge “a-2-6-5” without Position Indicator

FR #	VG	VF	XF	AU	CU	CH-CU (63)	GEM (65)	S-GEM (66)	RARITY
1324	–	125	170	200	450	650	1000	–	SCARCE

Red Back with Surcharge “a-2-6-5” with Position Indicators “1” and “a” on the Front

FR #	VG	VF	XF	AU	CU	CH-CU (63)	GEM (65)	S-GEM (66)	RARITY
1325	375	425	550	700	975	1200	2500	3400	RARE

Red Back with Surcharge “a-2-6-5” with Position Indicator “1” on the Front

FR #	VG	VF	XF	AU	CU	CH-CU (63)	GEM (65)	S-GEM (66)	RARITY
1326	–	135	195	220	350	650	1000	–	VERY SCARCE

Red Back with Surcharge “a-2-6-5” with Position Indicator “a” on the Front

FR #	VG	VF	XF	AU	CU	CH-CU (63)	GEM (65)	S-GEM (66)	RARITY
1327	–	135	195	275	395	595	1200	–	VERY SCARCE

Red Back with Autographed Signatures of Colby and Spinner

FR #	VG	VF	XF	AU	CU	CH-CU (63)	GEM (65)	S-GEM (66)	RARITY
1328	–	200	300	395	550	900	1700	1800	SCARCE

Red Back with Autographed Signatures of Allison and Spinner

FR #	VG	VF	XF	AU	CU	CH-CU (63)	GEM (65)	S-GEM (66)	RARITY
1329	–	250	350	450	700	1000	1800	2700	VERY SCARCE

Third Issue – Fifty Cent Fractional Currency: Spinner

Fr. 1329, Front

Fr. 1330, Front

Fr. 1331, Back

Red Back with Autographed Signatures of Allison and New

FR #	VG	VF	XF	AU	CU	CH-CU (63)	GEM (65)	S-GEM (66)	RARITY
1330	–	2000	2500	3200	4600	5700	8300	–	VERY RARE

Green Back without Surcharges, without Position Indicator

FR #	VG	VF	XF	AU	CU	CH-CU (63)	GEM (65)	S-GEM (66)	RARITY
1331	75	100	125	200	395	550	895	–	COMMON

Green Back without Surcharges, with Position Indicators "1" and "a" on the Front

FR #	VG	VF	XF	AU	CU	CH-CU (63)	GEM (65)	S-GEM (66)	RARITY
1332	–	120	175	250	425	675	1000	–	VERY SCARCE

Green Back without Surcharges, with Position Indicator "1" on the Front

FR #	VG	VF	XF	AU	CU	CH-CU (63)	GEM (65)	S-GEM (66)	RARITY
1333	75	100	135	200	325	595	895	–	SCARCE

Green Back without Surcharges, with Position Indicator "a" on the Front

FR #	VG	VF	XF	AU	CU	CH-CU (63)	GEM (65)	S-GEM (66)	RARITY
1334	–	95	110	200	375	595	900	–	SCARCE

Green Back with Surcharge "𝔄-2-6-5", without Position Indicator

FR #	VG	VF	XF	AU	CU	CH-CU (63)	GEM (65)	S-GEM (66)	RARITY
1335	–	95	125	300	450	550	995	–	VERY SCARCE

Third Issue – Fifty Cent Fractional Currency: Spinner

Fr. 1335, Back

Fr. 1339, Back
Type 2 Back

Green Back with Surcharge "𝔞-2-6-5", with Position Indicators "1" and "a"

FR #	VG	VF	XF	AU	CU	CH-CU (63)	GEM (65)	S-GEM (66)	RARITY
1336	–	2300	2700	3000	3600	5000	7900	–	VERY RARE

Green Back with Surcharge "𝔞-2-6-5", with Position Indicator "1" on the Front

FR #	VG	VF	XF	AU	CU	CH-CU (63)	GEM (65)	S-GEM (66)	RARITY
1337	–	150	250	350	750	1100	1600	–	RARE SLEEPER

Green Back with Surcharge "𝔞-2-6-5", with Position Indicator "a" on the Front

FR #	VG	VF	XF	AU	CU	CH-CU (63)	GEM (65)	S-GEM (66)	RARITY
1338	–	120	195	300	650	1000	1400	–	RARE SLEEPER

Green Back without Surcharges, without Position Indicator

FR #	VG	VF	XF	AU	CU	CH-CU (63)	GEM (65)	S-GEM (66)	RARITY
1339	–	100	155	225	325	425	800	1000	SCARCE

Green Back without Surcharges, with Position Indicators "1" and "a" on the Front

FR #	VG	VF	XF	AU	CU	CH-CU (63)	GEM (65)	S-GEM (66)	RARITY
1340	125	200	300	495	900	1200	1800	–	RARE

Green Back without Surcharges, with Position Indicator "1" on the Front

FR #	VG	VF	XF	AU	CU	CH-CU (63)	GEM (65)	S-GEM (66)	RARITY
1341	75	110	175	250	395	700	900	–	VERY SCARCE

Green Back without Surcharges, with Position Indicator "a" on the Front

FR #	VG	VF	XF	AU	CU	CH-CU (63)	GEM (65)	S-GEM (66)	RARITY
1342	75	125	225	395	550	750	1200	–	RARE

Third Issue – Fifty Cent Fractional Currency: Spinner

SIZE

46-48 mm x 113-115 mm. Printed in sheets of 12 notes.

WHAT TO LOOK FOR

Try to buy notes with good embossing, bright bronzing and clear, readable surcharges. Gems should have all these qualities, plus good margins, front and back.

Fr. 1324 GEMs can easily be found. Make sure surcharges are readable and not blurred. Should also have good embossing.

Fr. 1325 These notes are usually weakly printed on the upper left edges due to sheet position and may have some ink smears. The GEMs are difficult to find.

Fr. 1326 GEMs come up for sale about three to five times per year.

Fr. 1327 You should be able to find GEMs, but full, clear, complete inking is extremely rare.

Fr. 1328 Not a common note, but the most common of the Autographed Signature notes. GEMs can be found, usually with great embossing.

Fr. 1329 GEMs may be found with great margins.

Fr. 1330 Most of these are CU or better (90%). Estimates of 25 to 35 GEMs are known.

Fr. 1331 Comes well embossed most of the time.

Fr. 1332 GEMs do come up for sale. Mostly printed poorly in the upper left edges, as with many "1" and "a" notes.

Fr. 1333 Typically, the front centering is cut close to the left side or top.

Fr. 1334 GEMs can be found with great margins.

Fr. 1335 Maybe one out of ten are rated uncirculated or GEM.

Fr. 1336 Most of these are not CU. This is the hardest of the Spinner notes to find uncirculated, and therefore undervalued. Less than twenty known.

Fr. 1337 SLEEPER. An undervalued note. Much harder to find uncirculated or better than you might think.

Fr. 1338 SLEEPER. An undervalued note. Very hard to find AU or better.

Third Issue – Fifty Cent Fractional Currency: Spinner

Fr. 1339 GEMs can be found. Usually comes with great embossing.

Fr. 1340 These "1" and "a" Spinner Type two notes are partic ularly challenging to locate in uncirculated or bet ter. GEMs come up for sale maybe once or twice per year.

Fr. 1341 Most come cut close to the right or left sides. GEMs are hard to find.

Fr. 1342 Very hard to find CU or better.

Fourth Issue – Ten Cent Fractional Currency

Fr. 1257, Front

Fr. 1257, Back

Fr. 1258, Front

Fr. 1261, Front

Large Red Seal – 40 mm, Watermarked Paper, Pink Silk Fibers

FR #	VG	VF	XF	AU	CU	CH-CU (63)	GEM (65)	S-GEM (66)	RARITY
1257	–	50	70	90	125	250	495	695	VERY COMMON

Large Red Seal – 40 mm, Unwatermarked Paper, Pink Silk Fibers

FR #	VG	VF	XF	AU	CU	CH-CU (63)	GEM (65)	S-GEM (66)	RARITY
1258	–	55	95	125	175	250	450	–	SCARCE

Large Red Seal – 40 mm, Paper Has Violet Silk Fibers and Blue Front Right End

FR #	VG	VF	XF	AU	CU	CH-CU (63)	GEM (65)	S-GEM (66)	RARITY
1259	–	50	75	120	145	250	475	–	COMMON

Small Red Seal – 38 Mm, Paper Has Violet Silk Fibers and Blue Front Right End

FR #	VG	VF	XF	AU	CU	CH-CU (63)	GEM (65)	S-GEM (66)	RARITY
1261	–	55	95	125	175	250	450	–	SOMEWHAT COMMON

Former Number 1260 was not printed. The brown seal color variation may be due to a chemical change. This Friedberg number was delisted in the 6th edition (1968).

Former Number 1263 (No Seal). The seal may have been removed. I have not seen a genuine example.

Fourth Issue – Ten Cent Fractional Currency

4TH ISSUE PAPER

Due to the profusion of counterfeits, ordinary bank note paper was abandoned for the use of a more distinctive paper. The first notes of all denominations, issued from July through December 1869, were on paper showing watermark USUSUSUS and scattered pink fibers, both of which made it harder to counterfeit. The watermark was abandoned in just a few months because the paper tended to split along the lines of the watermarks. Also used for only a few months, was a type of paper with many scattered pink and red silk fibers. Next came a distinctive paper with localized blue stain.

Walter Breen, September 1974

Very few notes actually have the full "US" watermark. Many just have fragments of the watermark.

The following is from *Scientific American*, March 26th, 1870:

"In July 1866 letter patents were issued, through the Scientific America Patent Agency, to Jas. M. Wilcox, bank note manufacturer near Philadelphia, for an improvement in paper, to prevent counterfeiting."

"Mr. Wilcox has added a new feature to the paper that makes it so peculiar that it cannot be made by a hand process, or by cylinder machine, but only by a better-class fourdrinier machine and a special machine to locate the colored shreds. As this machinery exists only in his own mills, the public cannot duplicate this paper. The mill is guarded night and day by an armed force in pay of the government to prevent robbery."

"The shreds of red and blue silk are interwoven with the fibers of the paper, they are neither entirely under the surface nor entirely on the surface but both! A second process (with special machinery) is carried out to localize the blue fiber pulp into the paper, at one end of the sheets."

"The new 50¢ fractional currency Stanton note has the localized blue fibers occupying one end only of the note."

SIZE

45-47 mm x 78-80 mm. Printed in sheets of 16 notes.

WHAT TO LOOK FOR

True GEMS can be easily found for most of this issue.

Fourth Issue – Fifteen Cent Fractional Currency

Fr. 1267, Front

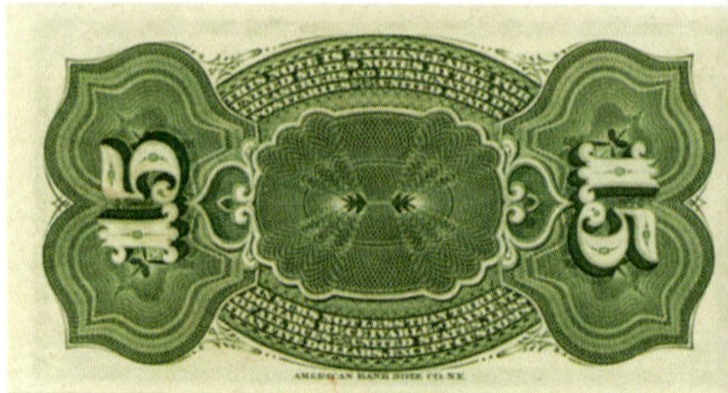

Fr. 1267, Back

Fr. 1269, Front. 40 mm seal

Fr. 1271, Front. 38 mm seal

Large Red Seal – 40 mm, Watermarked Paper, Pink Silk Fibers

FR #	VG	VF	XF	AU	CU	CH-CU (63)	GEM (65)	S-GEM (66)	RARITY
1267	50	75	125	175	250	325	595	–	SCARCE

Large Red Seal – 40 mm, Unwatermarked Paper, Pink Silk Fibers

FR #	VG	VF	XF	AU	CU	CH-CU (63)	GEM (65)	S-GEM (66)	RARITY
1268	–	500	700	900	1200	1600	*	–	RARE

Large Red Seal – 40 mm, Paper Has Violet Silk Fibers and Blue Front Right End

FR #	VG	VF	XF	AU	CU	CH-CU (63)	GEM (65)	S-GEM (66)	RARITY
1269	–	80	145	195	275	450	795	–	SCARCE

Small Red Seal – 38 Mm, Paper Has Violet Silk Fibers and Blue Front Right End

FR #	VG	VF	XF	AU	CU	CH-CU (63)	GEM (65)	S-GEM (66)	RARITY
1271	–	100	175	200	295	395	695	–	VERY SCARCE

* Have not seen any in GEM.

The former Number 1270 was not printed. Color variation may be due to a chemical change.

SIZE

45-47.5 mm x 88-90.25 mm. Printed in sheets of 12 notes.

WHAT TO LOOK FOR

You should check all Fr. 1268 notes for watermarks. Use a carbon tetrachloride test kit or other available non-harmful test kit available in all stamp stores or philatelic catalogs.

Fourth Issue – Twenty-five Cent Fractional Currency

Fr. 1301, Front

Fr. 1301, Back

Fr. 1307, Front

Large Red Seal – 40 mm, Watermarked Paper, Pink Silk Fibers

FR #	VG	VF	XF	AU	CU	CH-CU (63)	GEM (65)	S-GEM (66)	RARITY
1301	–	50	79	139	175	300	650	–	COMMON

Large Red Seal – 40 mm, Unwatermarked Paper, Pink Silk Fibers

FR #	VG	VF	XF	AU	CU	CH-CU (63)	GEM (65)	S-GEM (66)	RARITY
1302	–	50	100	155	225	325	700	–	COMMON

Large Red Seal – 40 mm, Paper with Blue Front Right End

FR #	VG	VF	XF	AU	CU	CH-CU (63)	GEM (65)	S-GEM (66)	RARITY
1303	–	55	125	250	325	450	795	–	VERY SCARCE

Small Red Seal – 38 Mm, Watermarked Paper with Blue Front Right End

FR #	VG	VF	XF	AU	CU	CH-CU (63)	GEM (65)	S-GEM (66)	RARITY
1307	–	60	100	200	300	425	700	–	SCARCE

The former Number 1305 was not printed. Color variation may be due to a chemical change.

SIZE

45-47 mm x 95-98 mm. Printed in sheets of 12 notes.

WHAT TO LOOK FOR

The Fr. 1303 is very hard to find in CHCU to GEM. Make sure to measure the size of the seal. Also, there should be no blue on the back. The color of the blue varies from light to medium-dark blue.

Fourth Issue – Fifty Cent Fractional Currency: Lincoln

Fr. 1374, Front

Fr. 1374, Back

Large Red Seal - 40 mm, Watermarked Paper - USUSUS

FR #	VG	VF	XF	AU	CU	CH-CU (63)	GEM (65)	S-GEM (66)	RARITY
1374	200	300	475	595	700	1200	2500	2700	*

* Common in VG through CU. Scarce in CHCU and True GEMS are rare, with maybe only one or two for sale per year.

Former Number 1375 does not exist. All known notes are watermarked.

SIZE

47 x 106 mm, the design 45-47 mm x 95-98 mm. Printed in sheets of 12 notes.

WHAT TO LOOK FOR

Most Lincoln notes are cut into the design at the bottom on the back. Try to find a Lincoln note with margins not touching the design. You should be able to find a nice CHCU with complete margins. True GEMs are rare, but they do come up at auctions. Also, check for center folds and processing, as many CHCU to GEM looking notes are in reality AUs.

Fourth Issue – Fifty Cent Fractional Currency: Stanton

Fr. 1376, Front

Fr. 1376, Back

Small Red Seal – 38 Mm, Paper Has Violet Silk Fibers and Blue Front Right End

FR #	VG	VF	XF	AU	CU	CH-CU (63)	GEM (65)	S-GEM (66)	RARITY
1376	75	110	145	190	350	550	1000	–	*

* Common in VG through CHCU. Scarce in GEM.

Former Number 1377 was not printed. Color variation may be due to a chemical change.

Former Number 1378 was once was said to be printed on plain paper. I have seen none in more than thirty years, nor have any of the other experts in the fractional field.

SIZE

45-47 mm x 102-104 mm. Printed in sheets of 12 notes.

WHAT TO LOOK FOR

Embossing of the Treasury Seal on GEMs should be strong and obvious. Any Stanton note with no embossing should be suspect.

Fourth Issue – Fifty Cent Fractional Currency: Dexter

Fr. 1379, Front

Fr. 1379, Back

Green Seal – Paper Has Light Violet Silk Fibers and Blue Front Right End

FR #	VG	VF	XF	AU	CU	CH-CU (63)	GEM (65)	S-GEM (66)	RARITY
1379	70	95	125	180	225	395	550	–	*

* Common in VG through CHCU. Scarce in GEM.

SIZE

51-53 mm x 94-96 mm. Printed in sheets of 12 notes.

WHAT TO LOOK FOR

Watch out for large pin holes in the upper front right-hand corner. Pin holes were caused when bundles were sewn together. GEMs can be found, but make sure that there are four good margins on both sides of the note. Most are cut close to the right or left hand side.

Fifth Issue - Ten Cent Fractional Currency

Fr. 1264, Front

Fr. 1265, Front

Long, Thin Key

Fr. 1264, Back

Short, Thick Key

Green Seal With Long, Thin Key – 5 mm

FR #	VG	VF	XF	AU	CU	CH-CU (63)	GEM (65)	S-GEM (66)	RARITY
1264		65	75	100	155	380	795		NOT THAT COMMON

Red Seal With Long, Thin Key – 5 mm

FR #	VG	VF	XF	AU	CU	CH-CU (63)	GEM (65)	S-GEM (66)	RARITY
1265		39	46	60	85	125	250		COMMON

Red Seal With Short, Thick Key – 4 mm

FR #	VG	VF	XF	AU	CU	CH-CU (63)	GEM (65)	S-GEM (66)	RARITY
1266		39	46	50	80	100	225		VERY COMMON

SIZE

50-52 mm x 80-82 mm.

WHAT TO LOOK FOR

GEMs of Fr. 1264 and Fr. 1265 are not that easy to find. Make sure your note has good margins on all four sides, both front and back. Check for pin holes in the upper right hand corner where bundles were sewn together.

Fifth Issue - Twenty-five Cent Fractional Currency

Fr. 1308, Front

Fr. 1309, Front

Fr. 1308, Back

Red Seal With Long, Thin Key – 5 mm

FR #	VG	VF	XF	AU	CU	CH-CU (63)	GEM (65)	S-GEM (66)	RARITY
1308		43	55	65	70	79	350	450	NOT THAT COMMON

Red Seal With Short, Thick Key – 4 mm

FR #	VG	VF	XF	AU	CU	CH-CU (63)	GEM (65)	S-GEM (66)	RARITY
1309		41	45	50	59	99	300	425	COMMON

SIZE

50-53 mm x 87-90 mm.

WHAT TO LOOK FOR

Check for pin holes in the upper right hand corner where bundles were sewn together.

Fifth Issue - Fifty Cent Fractional Currency

Fr. 1381, Front

Fr. 1381, Back

Red Seal, White Paper with Blue Fibers, Right End Back

FR #	VG	VF	XF	AU	CU	CH-CU (63)	GEM (65)	S-GEM (66)	RARITY
1381	25	35	75	90	125	250	595	700	VERY COMMON

SIZE

52-55 mm x 108-111 mm.

WHAT TO LOOK FOR

Crawford notes usually are cut close to the right or left side. Make sure that notes have good margins on all four sides, both front and back. Check for pin holes in the upper right hand corner where bundles were sewn together.

Part Four: Proofs

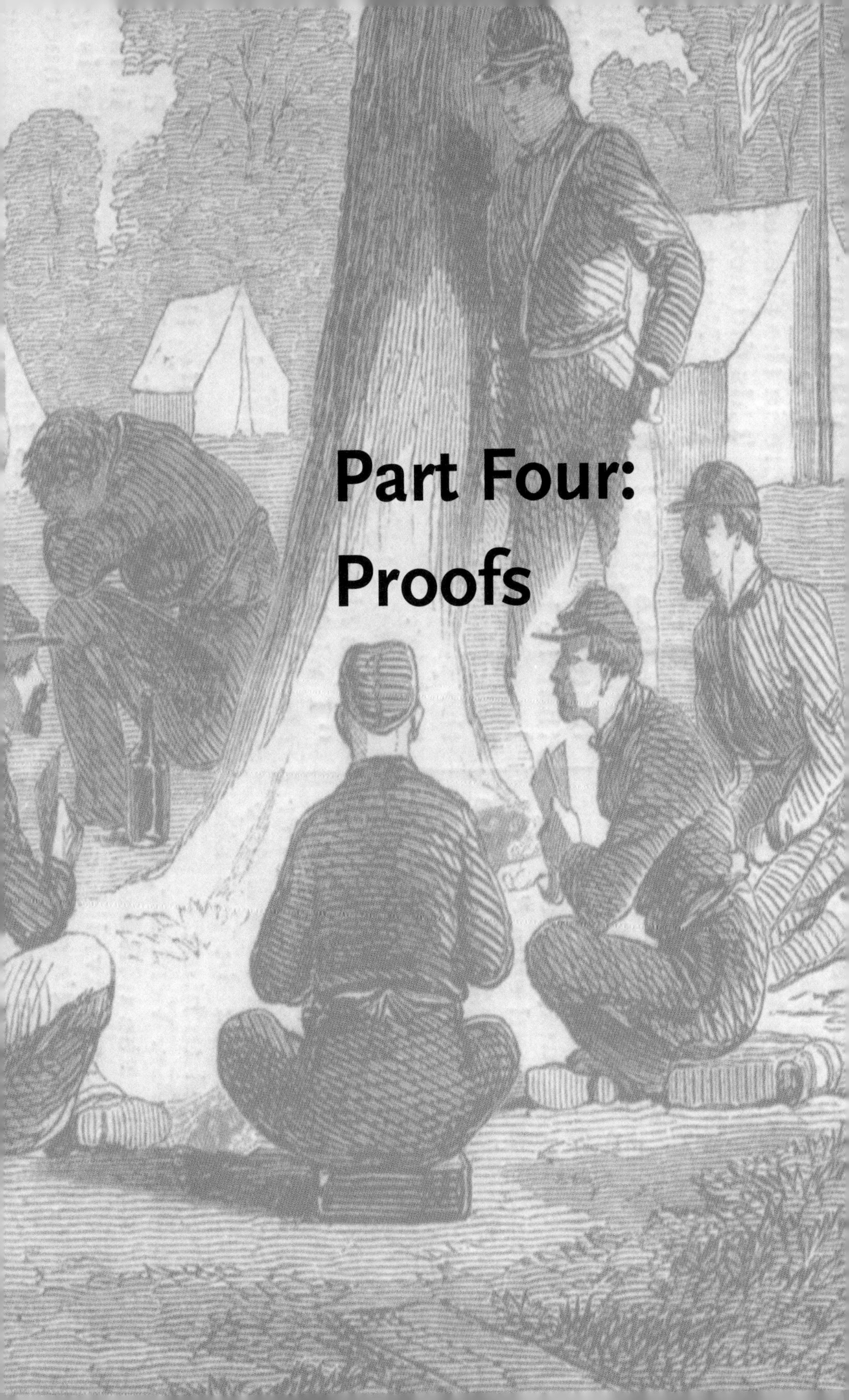

Proofs

HISTORY

Fractional Currency is the only field of currency collecting in which proofs notes (notes printed only on one side) from adopted designs, not intended for circulation, are available - and still affordable.

They are rare enough to be interesting and for now, undervalued. These are the real sleepers of the Fractional Currency market. For example, there were only 9,016 Grant/Sherman proof notes printed. As of 1884, only 3,513 were still outstanding. How many can be left today?

The proof notes are from the first three issues only. They come in narrow and wide margin varieties. Most of the narrow margin Proofs at one time were mounted on Fractional Currency Shields, so many of them show signs of glue stains and paper from the shield itself from when they were removed. Some may also have small edge tears from being removed from shields as well. The wide margin Proofs were sold in sets to the public starting in September, 1867, with the exception of the Grant/Sherman Proofs.

GRANT/SHERMAN Proofs

The real sleepers of the Fractional Currency Market The autographed (hand signed) Grant/Sherman notes seem to me to be one of the most overlooked Fractional Currency values. Not all Grant/Sherman notes have autographed signatures, but are still scarce. There were only 9,016 examples of all types of Grant/Shermans printed. As of 1884, only 3,513 were still outstanding. The notes were printed on very thin paper, which if mishandled over the last 140 plus years, would make the note an AU grade at best. Therefore, many of the wide margin examples over the years have been trimmed down to narrow margin examples usually to remove a corner tip fold or other signs of handling. The hand-signed notes (narrow or wide margin) are susceptible to getting burn holes in the signatures due to the acid in the ink or cracking in the thin paper as it has aged. Also, many examples (two fronts and two backs) are still on shields. Given this, how many Grant/Sherman Proofs can still be left in CHCU or better condition today?

HERE ARE ELEVEN DIFFERENT TYPES:

#1 & #2: Fr. 1272SP	Front printed signatures (Colby/Spinner) in both narrow and wide margin examples.
#3 & #4: Fr. 1272sp	Green back, both in narrow and wide margin examples.
#5: Fr. 1273sp	Front with autographed signatures of Colby and Spinner, narrow margin only (no wide margin examples known). These are found only on the green and pink shields. There are only a few known with no trace of being mounted on a shield (no glue/paper remnants). Maybe sixty known total. This includes twelve on known green shields and 25-27 on pink shields. There are only one or two GEMs known. Most of them are cut tight on the left or right hand side.
#6 & #7: Fr. 1274sp	Front with autographed signatures of Jeffries and Spinner, in both narrow and wide margin examples.
#8 & #9: Fr. 1275sp	Front with autographed signatures of Allison and Spinner, in both narrow and wide margin examples.
#10 & #11: Fr. 1273-75sp	Red back, in both narrow and wide margin.

The most common Grant/Sherman (if any can be called common) are the Fr. 1272sp narrow margin front and the narrow margin green back. Also, the narrow margin red backs (Fr. 1273-75sp). The Fr. 1274sp and the Fr. 1275sp narrow margin fronts are the scarcest. They appear in auctions maybe four or five times per year. Most are mounted on shields withnormal glue and paper remnants (or mounting marks on the back). The few GEMs that do come up are from cut down wide margin examples. This is one of the reasons why wide margin Fr. 1274sp and Fr. 1275sp fronts are very scarce in GEM condition. These may appear in only two or three auction every year.

The 15¢ Grant/Sherman notes were printed only as proofs. Although several plates were made for regular production (with 12 notes per plate), no regular issue notes were made. One 8 subject plate (plate #1) was for wide margin backs, and two 8 subject plates (plates #2 & #3) were for the fronts, all being wide margin.

Most of the Uncirculated or better Grant/Sherman notes are just staying in collections. Consequently, not that many GEMs come-up for sale. With less and less supply becoming available and the ever increasing demand, prices have no where to go but up. The prices for Grant/Sherman Proofs have surpassed the peak prices for 1981. They will continue to go up as more and more sets are put together. Soon all the GEM Grant/Sherman examples will be in collections. With many new and young collectors of fractional currency, these notes will not be available for many years to come. Do not wait. Buy your Grant/Sherman notes now before they are all gone.

Wide-margin proofs were cut by hand, therefore the dimensions may differ by just a few millimeters. If the dimensions (from frame line to cutting line) are substantially less (say 5 to 10 millimeters), then the note should be considered as *trimmed*. These trimmed notes should be worth much less then those that are fully wide margined.

The width of the margins varies based upon the note, as not all engravings are the same size. *This distance is measured from the frame line of the engraving to the cutting line on the sheet*. The sheet layouts in the 3rd issue 15¢ and 25¢ proof notes resulted in a variation of distances between the frame line and the cutting line.

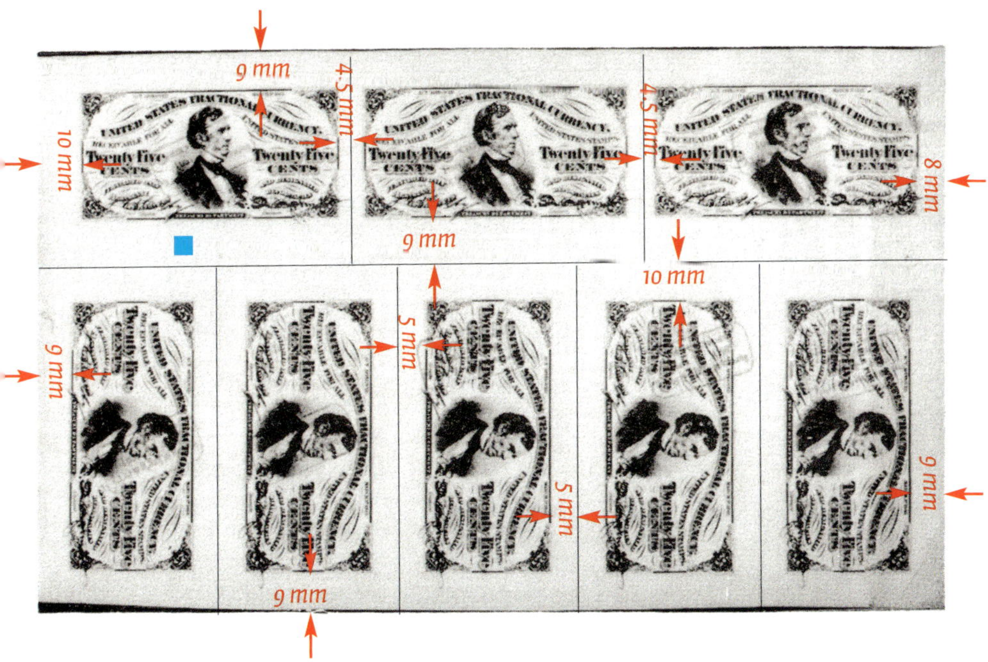

■ Indicates Plate Number Position

Proofs: First Issue – Five Cent

Fr. 1231spwmf, Front. Wide Margins

Fr. 1231spwmb, Back. Wide Margins

Front with Narrow Margins

FR #	VG	VF	XF	AU	CU	CH-CU (63)	GEM (65)	S-GEM (66)	RARITY
1231spnmf	–	–	–	75	125	175	395	500	COMMON

Front with Wide Margins

FR #	VG	VF	XF	AU	CU	CH-CU (63)	GEM (65)	S-GEM (66)	RARITY
1231spwmf	–	–	–	175	300	450	550	950	SCARCE SLEEPER

Back with Narrow Margins

FR #	VG	VF	XF	AU	CU	CH-CU (63)	GEM (65)	S-GEM (66)	RARITY
1231spnmb	–	–	–	75	125	200	395	500	COMMON

Back with Wide Margins

FR #	VG	VF	XF	AU	CU	CH-CU (63)	GEM (65)	S-GEM (66)	RARITY
1231spwmb	–	–	–	175	600	450	550	950	SCARCE SLEEPER

SIZE

Narrow Margins: 44-45 mm by 63-65 mm.

Wide Margins: 64-67 mm by 96-99 mm.

WIDE MARGIN BORDER *(Frame Line to Cutting Line)*

Front: 11.5 mm by 16.5 mm.

Back: 11.75 mm by 16.5 mm.

WHAT TO LOOK FOR

On wide margin examples, a corner fold not into the design, still makes it an AU note. With narrow margin examples, buy those without glue or shield paper remnants on the back.

Proofs: First Issue – Ten Cent

Fr. 1243spwmf, Front. Wide Margins

Fr. 1243spwmb, Back. Wide Margins

Front with Narrow Margins

FR #	VG	VF	XF	AU	CU	CH-CU (63)	GEM (65)	S-GEM (66)	RARITY
1243spnmf	–	–	–	75	125	200	395	500	COMMON

Front with Wide Margins

FR #	VG	VF	XF	AU	CU	CH-CU (63)	GEM (65)	S-GEM (66)	RARITY
1243spwmf	–	–	–	175	300	450	550	950	SCARCE

Back with Narrow Margins

FR #	VG	VF	XF	AU	CU	CH-CU (63)	GEM (65)	S-GEM (66)	RARITY
1243spnmb	–	–	–	75	125	200	395	500	COMMON

Back with Wide Margins

FR #	VG	VF	XF	AU	CU	CH-CU (63)	GEM (65)	S-GEM (66)	RARITY
1243spwmb	–	–	–	175	300	450	650	950	SCARCE

SIZE

Narrow Margins: 44-45 mm by 63-65 mm.
Wide Margins: 64-67 mm by 96-99 mm.

WIDE MARGIN BORDER *(Frame Line to Cutting Line)*
Front: 11.5/12 mm by 16 mm.
Back: 12 mm by 16 mm.

WHAT TO LOOK FOR

On wide margin examples, a corner fold not into the design still makes it an AU note. With narrow margin examples, buy those without glue or shield paper remnants on the back.

Proofs: First Issue – Twenty-five Cent

Fr. 1282spwmf, Front. Wide Margins

Fr. 1282spwmb, Back. Wide Margins

Front with Narrow Margins

FR #	VG	VF	XF	AU	CU	CH-CU (63)	GEM (65)	S-GEM (66)	RARITY
1282spnmf	–	–	–	75	125	200	395	500	SOMEWHAT COMMON

Front with Wide Margins

FR #	VG	VF	XF	AU	CU	CH-CU (63)	GEM (65)	S-GEM (66)	RARITY
1282spwmf	–	–	–	175	300	450	650	750	SCARCE

Back with Narrow Margins

FR #	VG	VF	XF	AU	CU	CH-CU (63)	GEM (65)	S-GEM (66)	RARITY
1282spnmb	–	–	–	75	125	200	395	500	COMMON

Back with Wide Margins

FR #	VG	VF	XF	AU	CU	CH-CU (63)	GEM (65)	S-GEM (66)	RARITY
1282spwmb	–	–	–	175	300	450	650	950	SCARCE

SIZE

Narrow Margins: 47-48 mm by 77-78 mm.
Wide Margins: 64-67 mm by 97-100 mm.

WIDE MARGIN BORDER *(Frame Line to Cutting Line)*

Front: 10 mm by 10 mm.
Back: 10 mm by 10 mm.

WHAT TO LOOK FOR

On wide margin examples, a corner fold not into the design, still makes it an AU note. With narrow margin examples, buy those without glue or shield paper remnants on the back.

Proofs: First Issue – Fifty Cent

Fr. 1313spwmf, Front. Wide Margins

Fr. 1313spwmb, Back. Wide Margins

Front with Narrow Margins

FR #	VG	VF	XF	AU	CU	CH-CU (63)	GEM (65)	S-GEM (66)	RARITY
1313spnmf	–	–	–	75	125	200	395	500	SOMEWHAT COMMON

Front with Wide Margins

FR #	VG	VF	XF	AU	CU	CH-CU (63)	GEM (65)	S-GEM (66)	RARITY
1313spwmf	–	–	–	225	425	600	100	1250	SCARCE

Back with Narrow Margins

FR #	VG	VF	XF	AU	CU	CH-CU (63)	GEM (65)	S-GEM (66)	RARITY
313spnmb	–	–	–	75	125	200	395	500	SCARCE SLEEPER

Back with Wide Margins

FR #	VG	VF	XF	AU	CU	CH-CU (63)	GEM (65)	S-GEM (66)	RARITY
313spwmb	–	–	–	175	300	550	900	1000	SCARCE

SIZE

Narrow Margins: 47-48 mm by 64-67 mm.
Wide Margins: 77-78 mm by 97-100 mm.

WIDE MARGIN BORDER *(Frame Line to Cutting Line)*

Front: 10 mm by 10 mm.
Back: 10 mm by 10 mm.

WHAT TO LOOK FOR

On wide margin examples, a corner fold not into the design, still makes it an AU note. With narrow margin examples, buy those without glue or shield paper remnants on the back.

Proofs: Second Issue – Five Cent

Fr. 1232spwmf, Front. Wide Margins

Fr. 1232spwmb, Back. Wide Margins

Front with Narrow Margins

FR #	VG	VF	XF	AU	CU	CH-CU (63)	GEM (65)	S-GEM (66)	RARITY
1232spnmf	–	–	–	75	175	200	395	500	COMMON

Front with Wide Margins

FR #	VG	VF	XF	AU	CU	CH-CU (63)	GEM (65)	S-GEM (66)	RARITY
1232spwmf	–	–	–	175	300	450	650	750	VERY SCARCE

Back with Narrow Margins

FR #	VG	VF	XF	AU	CU	CH-CU (63)	GEM (65)	S-GEM (66)	RARITY
1232spnmb	–	–	–	75	175	200	395	500	COMMON

Back with Wide Margins

FR #	VG	VF	XF	AU	CU	CH-CU (63)	GEM (65)	S-GEM (66)	RARITY
1232spwmb	–	–	–	175	300	450	650	750	VERY SCARCE RARE IN GEM

SIZE

Narrow Margins: 46-49 mm by 64-68 mm.
Wide Margins: 64-68 mm by 96-99 mm.

WIDE MARGIN BORDER *(Frame Line to Cutting Line)*

Front: 9 mm by 16.5 mm.
Back: 10 mm by 17 mm.

WHAT TO LOOK FOR

Buy fronts that have bright bronzing. Buy backs that have good, deep, rich color and bright bronzing.

Proofs: Second Issue – Ten Cent

Fr. 1244spwmf, Front Wide Margins

Fr. 1244spwmb, Back. Wide Margins

Front with Narrow Margins

FR #	VG	VF	XF	AU	CU	CH-CU (63)	GEM (65)	S-GEM (66)	RARITY
1244spnmf	–	–	–	75	125	200	395	500	COMMON

Front with Wide Margins

FR #	VG	VF	XF	AU	CU	CH-CU (63)	GEM (65)	S-GEM (66)	RARITY
1244spwmf	–	–	–	175	300	450	650	750	VERY SCARCE

Back with Narrow Margins

FR #	VG	VF	XF	AU	CU	CH-CU (63)	GEM (65)	S-GEM (66)	RARITY
1244spnmb	–	–		75	125	200	395	500	COMMON

Back with Wide Margins

FR #	VG	VF	XF	AU	CU	CH-CU (63)	GEM (65)	S-GEM (66)	RARITY
1244spwmb	–	–	–	175	300	450	650	750	VERY SCARCE

SIZE

Narrow Margins: 46-49 mm by 64-68 mm.
Wide Margins: 64-68 mm by 96-99 mm.

WIDE MARGIN BORDER *(Frame Line to Cutting Line)*

Front: 9 mm by 16.5 mm.
Back: 10 mm by 17 mm.

WHAT TO LOOK FOR

Buy fronts that have bright bronzing. Buy backs that have good, deep, rich color and bright bronzing.

Proofs: Second Issue – Twenty-five Cent

Fr. 1283spwmf, Front. Wide Margins

Fr. 1283spwmb, Back. Wide Margins

Front with Narrow Margins

FR #	VG	VF	XF	AU	CU	CH-CU (63)	GEM (65)	S-GEM (66)	RARITY
1283spnmf	–	–	–	75	125	200	395	500	COMMON

Front with Wide Margins

FR #	VG	VF	XF	AU	CU	CH-CU (63)	GEM (65)	S-GEM (66)	RARITY
1283spwmf	--	–	–	175	300	450	650	750	VERY SCARCE

Back with Narrow Margins

FR #	VG	VF	XF	AU	CU	CH-CU (63)	GEM (65)	S-GEM (66)	RARITY
1283nmb	–	–	–	75	125	200	395	500	COMMON

Back with Wide Margins

FR #	VG	VF	XF	AU	CU	CH-CU (63)	GEM (65)	S-GEM (66)	RARITY
1283wmb	–	–	–	175	300	450	650	750	VERY SCARCE RARE IN GEM

SIZE

Narrow Margins: 46-49 mm by 64-68 mm.
Wide Margins: 64-68 mm by 96-99 mm.

WIDE MARGIN BORDER *(Frame Line to Cutting Line)*

Front: 9 mm by 16.5 mm.
Back: 10 mm by 17 mm.

WHAT TO LOOK FOR

Buy fronts that have bright bronzing. Buy backs that have good, deep, rich color and bright bronzing.

Proofs: Second Issue – Fifty Cent

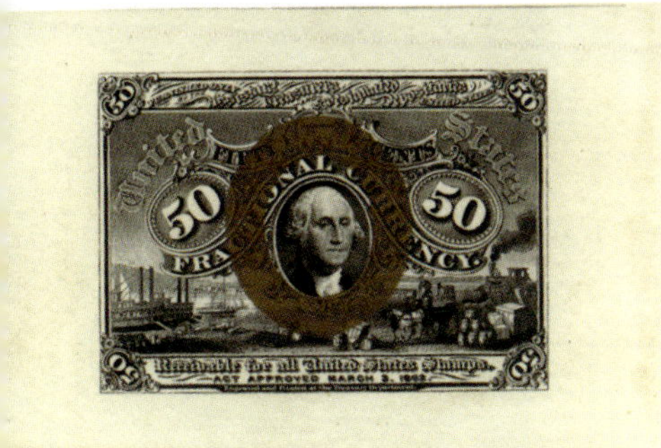

Fr. 1314spwmf, Front. Wide Margins

Fr. 1314spwmb, Back. Wide Margins

Front with Narrow Margins

FR #	VG	VF	XF	AU	CU	CH-CU (63)	GEM (65)	S-GEM (66)	RARITY
1314spnmf	–	–	–	75	125	200	395	500	SOMEWHAT COMMON

Front with Wide Margins

FR #	VG	VF	XF	AU	CU	CH-CU (63)	GEM (65)	S-GEM (66)	RARITY
1314spwmf	–	–	–	200	350	500	700	900	VERY SCARCE

Back with Narrow Margins

FR #	VG	VF	XF	AU	CU	CH-CU (63)	GEM (65)	S-GEM (66)	RARITY
1314spnmb	–	–	–	75	125	200	395	500	SOMEWHAT COMMON

Back with Wide Margins

FR #	VG	VF	XF	AU	CU	CH-CU (63)	GEM (65)	S-GEM (66)	RARITY
1314spwmb	–	–	–	300	500	650	900	1400	VERY SCARCE RARE IN GEM

SIZE

Narrow Margins: 46-49 mm by 64-68 mm.
Wide Margins: 64-68 mm by 96-100 mm.

WIDE MARGIN BORDER *(Frame Line to Cutting Line)*

Front: 9 mm by 16.5 mm.
Back: 10 mm by 17 mm.

WHAT TO LOOK FOR

Buy fronts that have bright bronzing. Buy backs that have good, deep, rich color and bright bronzing.

Proofs: Third Issue – Three Cent

Fr. 1226spwmf, Front. Wide Margins

Fr. 1227spwmf, Front. Wide Margins

Fr. 1226spwmb, Back. Wide Margins

Front with Narrow Margins – Light Background to Portrait

FR #	VG	VF	XF	AU	CU	CH-CU (63)	GEM (65)	S-GEM (66)	RARITY
1226spnmf	–	–	–	75	125	200	395	500	COMMON

Front with Wide Margins – Light Background to Portrait

FR #	VG	VF	XF	AU	CU	CH-CU (63)	GEM (65)	S-GEM (66)	RARITY
1226spwmf	–	–	–	5000	7000	9000	12000	–	VERY RARE 3 KNOWN

Front with Narrow Margins – Dark Background to Portrait

FR #	VG	VF	XF	AU	CU	CH-CU (63)	GEM (65)	S-GEM (66)	RARITY
1227spnmf	–	–	–	75	125	200	395	500	SOMEWHAT COMMON

Front with Wide Margins – Dark Background to Portrait

FR #	VG	VF	XF	AU	CU	CH-CU (63)	GEM (65)	S-GEM (66)	RARITY
1227spwmf	–	–	–	175	450	550	700	1200	SCARCE

Back with Narrow Margins

FR #	VG	VF	XF	AU	CU	CH-CU (63)	GEM (65)	S-GEM (66)	RARITY
1226spwmb	–	–	–	250	350	450	650	850	COMMON

Back with Wide Margins

FR #	VG	VF	XF	AU	CU	CH-CU (63)	GEM (65)	S-GEM (66)	RARITY
1226spnmb	–	–	–	100	195	250	395		SCARCE

SIZE

Narrow Margins: 39-40 mm by 64-65 mm.

Wide Margins: 62-64 mm by 95-98 mm.

WIDE MARGIN BORDER *(Frame Line to Cutting Line)*

Front: 12 mm by 16 mm.

Back: 12 mm by 17 mm.

WHAT TO LOOK FOR

If someone offers you a wide margin, Fr. 1226 proof, light background, be skeptical. There are only three known. Although someday, another one may turn up. The three known are all in collections not going to be sold any time soon. Check photos on previous page. Any note with a corner fold is an AU. Many are sold as CU because the fold may not encroach the design, but a fold is still a fold.

Proofs: Third Issue – Five Cent

Fr. 1236spwmf, Front. Wide Margins

Fr. 1236spwmb, Back. Wide Margins

Fr. 1238spwmf, Back. Wide Margins

Front with Narrow Margins

FR #	VG	VF	XF	AU	CU	CH-CU (63)	GEM (65)	S-GEM (66)	RARITY
1236spnmf	–	–	–	100	195	250	395	–	COMMON

Front with Wide Margins

FR #	VG	VF	XF	AU	CU	CH-CU (63)	GEM (65)	S-GEM (66)	RARITY
1236spwmf	–	–	–	250	350	450	700	–	SCARCE

Red Back with Narrow Margins

FR #	VG	VF	XF	AU	CU	CH-CU (63)	GEM (65)	S-GEM (66)	RARITY
1236spnmb	–	–	–	100	195	250	395	–	SOMEWHAT COMMON

Red Back with Wide Margins

FR #	VG	VF	XF	AU	CU	CH-CU (63)	GEM (65)	S-GEM (66)	RARITY
1236spwmb	–	–	–	200	395	550	750	–	SCARCE

Green Back with Narrow Margins

FR #	VG	VF	XF	AU	CU	CH-CU (63)	GEM (65)	S-GEM (66)	RARITY
1238spnmb	–	–	–	100	125	250	395	–	COMMON

Green Back with Wide Margins

FR #	VG	VF	XF	AU	CU	CH-CU (63)	GEM (65)	S-GEM (66)	RARITY
1238spwmb	–	–	–	195	295	395	700	–	SCARCE

SIZE

Narrow Margins: 47-49 mm by 79-81 mm.

Wide Margins: 60-63 mm by 92-99 mm.

WIDE MARGIN BORDER *(Frame Line to Cutting Line)*

Front: 9 mm by 17 mm.

Back: 10 mm by 18 mm.

WHAT TO LOOK FOR

On wide margin examples, the margins are narrower on the top and bottom than on the sides. Backs should have good, deep, rich color in red or green and bright bronzing.

Proofs: Third Issue – Ten Cent

Fr. 1251spwmf, Front. Wide Margins

Fr. 1253spwmf, Front. Wide Margins

Fr. 1254spwmf, Front. Wide Margins

Front with Narrow Margins, with Printed Signatures of Colby and Spinner

FR #	VG	VF	XF	AU	CU	CH-CU (63)	GEM (65)	S-GEM (66)	RARITY
1251spnmf	–	–	–	100	125	250	395	–	COMMON

Front with Wide Margins, with Printed Signatures of Colby and Spinner

FR #	VG	VF	XF	AU	CU	CH-CU (63)	GEM (65)	S-GEM (66)	RARITY
1251spwmf	–	–	–	225	325	450	700	–	SOMEWHAT COMMON

Front with Narrow Margins, with Autographed Signatures of Colby and Spinner

FR #	VG	VF	XF	AU	CU	CH-CU (63)	GEM (65)	S-GEM (66)	RARITY
1253spnmf	–	–	–	100	190	295	450	–	SCARCE

Front with Wide Margins, with Autographed Signatures of Colby and Spinner

FR #	VG	VF	XF	AU	CU	CH-CU (63)	GEM (65)	S-GEM (66)	RARITY
1253spwmf	–	–	–	250	500	700	900	1100	VERY SCARCE

Front with Narrow Margins, with Autographed Signatures of Jeffries and Spinner

FR #	VG	VF	XF	AU	CU	CH-CU (63)	GEM (65)	S-GEM (66)	RARITY
1254spnmf	–	–	–	295	395	495	750	–	VERY SCARCE

Proofs: Third Issue – Ten Cent

Fr. 1251spwmb, Back. Wide Margins

Fr. 1255spwmb, Back. Wide Margins

Front with Wide Margins, with Autographed Signatures of Jeffries and Spinner

FR #	VG	VF	XF	AU	CU	CH-CU (63)	GEM (65)	S-GEM (66)	RARITY
1254spwmf	–	–	–	3000	3900	6000	9000	–	VERY RARE 8 KNOWN

Red Back with Narrow Margins

FR #	VG	VF	XF	AU	CU	CH-CU (63)	GEM (65)	S-GEM (66)	RARITY
251-4spnmb	–	–	–	100	150	250	395	–	COMMON

Red Back with Wide Margins

FR #	VG	VF	XF	AU	CU	CH-CU (63)	GEM (65)	S-GEM (66)	RARITY
251-4spwmb	–	–	–	295	305	495	750	–	SOMEWHAT COMMON

Green Back with Narrow Margins

FR #	VG	VF	XF	AU	CU	CH-CU (63)	GEM (65)	S-GEM (66)	RARITY
1255spnmb	–	–	–	100	150	250	395	–	COMMON

Green Back with Wide Margins

FR #	VG	VF	XF	AU	CU	CH-CU (63)	GEM (65)	S-GEM (66)	RARITY
1255spwmb	–	–	–	200	325	450	700	–	SCARCE

SIZE

Narrow Margins: 47-48 mm by 80-82 mm.

Wide Margins: 60-68 mm by 95-100 mm.

WIDE MARGIN BORDER *(Frame Line to Cutting Line)*

Front: 9 mm by 9 mm.

Back: 10 mm by 10 mm.

WHAT TO LOOK FOR

Check the autographed examples for “burn holes” (where the acid in the ink has burned through the thin paper). Examples damaged in this way are worth about half of the stated values. Backs should have good, deep, rich color in red or green.

Proofs: Third Issue – Fifteen Cent: Grant/Sherman

Fr. 1272spwmf, Front. Wide Margins

Fr. 1273spnmf, Front. Narrow Margins ONLY

Fr. 1274spwmf, Front. Wide Margins

Fr. 1275spwmf, Front. Wide Margins

Proofs: Third Issue – Fifteen Cent: Grant/Sherman

Fr. 1276spwmf, Front. Wide Margins

Fr. 1272spwmb, Back. Wide Margins

Fr. 1273spwmb, Back. Wide Margins

MILT 3E15E.1, Cardboard Essay.
Unique. Note: No Flourish Lines

Proofs: Third Issue – Fifteen Cent: Grant/Sherman

MILT 3P15F.1a, Strip of 3. Unique

Proofs: Third Issue – Fifteen Cent: Grant/Sherman

Front with Narrow Margins, with Printed Signatures of Colby and Spinner

FR #	VG	VF	XF	AU	CU	CH-CU (63)	GEM (65)	S-GEM (66)	RARITY
1272spnmf	–	–	300	595	750	1100	1600	2000	SCARCE

Front with Wide Margins, with Printed Signatures of Colby and Spinner

FR #	VG	VF	XF	AU	CU	CH-CU (63)	GEM (65)	S-GEM (66)	RARITY
1272spwmf	–	–	500	595	750	2100	3000	3600	VERY SCARCE

Green Back with Narrow Margins

FR #	VG	VF	XF	AU	CU	CH-CU (63)	GEM (65)	S-GEM (66)	RARITY
1272spnmb	–	–	125	200	300	450	595	700	COMMON

Green Back with Wide Margins

FR #	VG	VF	XF	AU	CU	CH-CU (63)	GEM (65)	S-GEM (66)	RARITY
1272spwmb	–	–	250	375	425	750	1000	1400	SCARCE

Front with Narrow Margins, with Autographed Signatures of Colby and Spinner

FR #	VG	VF	XF	AU	CU	CH-CU (63)	GEM (65)	S-GEM (66)	RARITY
1273spnmf	–	–	–	1400	2500	3600	5900	7000	RARE

Front with Narrow Margins, with Autographed Signatures of Jeffries and Spinner

FR #	VG	VF	XF	AU	CU	CH-CU (63)	GEM (65)	S-GEM (66)	RARITY
1274spnmf	–	–	–	595	795	1200	1900	2500	VERY SCARCE

Front with Wide Margins, with Autographed Signatures of Jeffries and Spinner

FR #	VG	VF	XF	AU	CU	CH-CU (63)	GEM (65)	S-GEM (66)	RARITY
1274spwmf	–	–	–	700	895	2300	3200	3900	SOMEWHAT RARE

Front with Narrow Margins, with Autographed Signatures of Allison and Spinner

FR #	VG	VF	XF	AU	CU	CH-CU (63)	GEM (65)	S-GEM (66)	RARITY
1275spnmf	–	–	–	595	750	1100	2900	3700	VERY SCARCE

Front with Wide Margins, with Autographed Signatures of Allison and Spinner

FR #	VG	VF	XF	AU	CU	CH-CU (63)	GEM (65)	S-GEM (66)	RARITY
1275spwmf	–	–	–	795	995	2600	3400	4300	RARE

Red Back with Narrow Margins

FR #	VG	VF	XF	AU	CU	CH-CU (63)	GEM (65)	S-GEM (66)	RARITY
1273spnmb	–	–	200	250	395	450	700	900	COMMON

Red Back with Wide Margins

FR #	VG	VF	XF	AU	CU	CH-CU (63)	GEM (65)	S-GEM (66)	RARITY
1273spwmb	–	–	350	900	1800	2300	2700	3000	VERY SCARCE RARE IN GEM

Proofs: Third Issue – Fifteen Cent: Grant/Sherman

Front with Narrow Margins, with No Signatures

FR #	VG	VF	XF	AU	CU	CH-CU (63)	GEM (65)	S-GEM (66)	RARITY
1276spnmf	–	–	–	–	–	18K	–	–	1 KNOWN

Front with Wide Margins, with No Signatures

FR #	VG	VF	XF	AU	CU	CH-CU (63)	GEM (65)	S-GEM (66)	RARITY
1276spwmb	–	–	–	–	–	30K	–	*	1 KNOWN

*Last time it sold in GEM was at the Milt Friedberg sale, 1/20/97 for $4,100.00. Today it would bring up to ten times that amount.

SIZE

Narrow Margins: 46-50 mm by 88-92 mm.

Wide Margins: 65-75 mm by 109-117 mm.

WIDE MARGIN BORDER *(Frame Line to Cutting Line)*

Margin sizes vary based upon sheet position (see page 101).

WHAT TO LOOK FOR

Most Fr. 1273 spnm are cut close or into the design. Also, most have remnants of shield on the back. Try to buy one that is not cut into the design. Check the autograph notes for "burn holes" (where the acid in the ink has burned through the thin paper. They are worth about half of the stated value.

Proofs: Third Issue – Twenty-five Cent

Fr. 1291spwmf, Front. Wide Margins

Fr. 1291spwmb, Back. Wide Margins

Front with Narrow Margins

FR #	VG	VF	XF	AU	CU	CH-CU (63)	GEM (65)	S-GEM (66)	RARITY
1294spnmf	–	–	–	100	125	250	395	–	COMMON

Front with Wide Margins

FR #	VG	VF	XF	AU	CU	CH-CU (63)	GEM (65)	S-GEM (66)	RARITY
1294spwmf	–	–	–	225	325	500	700	–	SCARCE

Red Back with Narrow Margins

FR #	VG	VF	XF	AU	CU	CH-CU (63)	GEM (65)	S-GEM (66)	RARITY
1291spnmb	–	–	–	110	150	275	425	–	COMMON

Red Back with Wide Margins

FR #	VG	VF	XF	AU	CU	CH-CU (63)	GEM (65)	S-GEM (66)	RARITY
1291spwmb	–	–	–	225	350	550	700	900	SCARCE

Proofs: Third Issue – Twenty-five Cent

Fr. 1294spwmb, Back. Wide Margins

Green Back with Narrow Margins

FR #	VG	VF	XF	AU	CU	CH-CU (63)	GEM (65)	S-GEM (66)	RARITY
1294spnmb	–	–	–	100	125	250	395	–	COMMON

Green Back with Wide Margins

FR #	VG	VF	XF	AU	CU	CH-CU (63)	GEM (65)	S-GEM (66)	RARITY
1294spwmb	–	–	–	225	350	550	700	–	SCARCE

SIZE

Narrow Margins: 46-48 mm by 95-97 mm.
Wide Margins: 60-65 mm by 110-116 mm.

WIDE MARGIN BORDER *(Frame Line to Cutting Line)*

Margin sizes vary based upon sheet position. See page 101.

WHAT TO LOOK FOR

The Fr. 1294spnm face is found with the word "SPECIMEN" inverted on the back of all the ones I've seen. Both red and green examples should have strong color.

Proofs: Third Issue – Fifty Cent: Justice

Fr. 1343spwmf, Front. Wide Margins

Fr. 1355spwmf, Front. Wide Margins

Front with Narrow Margins, with Printed Signatures of Colby and Spinner

FR #	VG	VF	XF	AU	CU	CH-CU (63)	GEM (65)	S GEM (66)	RARITY
1343spnmf	–	–	–	100	125	250	395	–	SOMEWHAT COMMON

Front with Wide Margins, with Printed Signatures of Colby and Spinner

FR #	VG	VF	XF	AU	CU	CH-CU (63)	GEM (65)	S-GEM (66)	RARITY
1343spwmf	–	–	–	225	350	550	750	–	SCARCE

Front with Narrow Margins, with Autographed Signatures of Colby and Spinner

FR #	VG	VF	XF	AU	CU	CH-CU (63)	GEM (65)	S-GEM (66)	RARITY
1355spnmf	–	–	–	250	350	500	900	–	SCARCE

Front with Wide Margins, with Autographed Signatures of Colby and Spinner

FR #	VG	VF	XF	AU	CU	CH-CU (63)	GEM (65)	S-GEM (66)	RARITY
1355spwmf	–	–	–	500	700	900	1200	1600	VERY SCARCE

Front with Narrow Margins, with Autographed Signatures of Jeffries and Spinner

FR #	VG	VF	XF	AU	CU	CH-CU (63)	GEM (65)	S-GEM (66)	RARITY
1357spnmf	–	–	–	300	500	700	900	–	VERY SCARCE

Front with Wide Margins, with Autographed Signatures of Jeffries and Spinner

FR #	VG	VF	XF	AU	CU	CH-CU (63)	GEM (65)	S-GEM (66)	RARITY
1357spwmf	–	–	–	5900	9000	12000	–	–	RARE

Proofs: Third Issue – Fifty Cent: Justice

Fr. 1357spwmf, Front. Wide Margins

SIZE

Narrow Margins: 46-51 mm by 113-115 mm.
Wide Margins: 59-64 mm by 127-137 mm.

WIDE MARGIN BORDER *(Frame Line to Cutting Line)*

Front: 9 mm by 11 mm.
Back: 10 mm by 14 mm.

WHAT TO LOOK FOR

Check the autographed notes for "burn holes' (where the acid in the ink has burned through the thin paper). These notes are worth about half, or less, than the stated values.

NOTE: Fr. 1357spnmf and Fr. 1357spwmf only come as Proofs.

Proofs: Third Issue – Fifty Cent: Spinner

Fr. 1324spwmf, Front. Wide Margins

Fr. 1329spwmf, Front. Wide Margins

Front with Narrow Margins, with Printed Signatures of Colby and Spinner

FR #	VG	VF	XF	AU	CU	CH-CU (63)	GEM (65)	S-GEM (66)	RARITY
1324spnmf	–	–	–	100	200	295	395	595	SCARCE

Front with Wide Margins, with Printed Signatures of Colby and Spinner

FR #	VG	VF	XF	AU	CU	CH-CU (63)	GEM (65)	S-GEM (66)	RARITY
1324spwmf	–	–	–	225	350	450	700	–	SCARCE

Front with Narrow Margins, with Autographed Signatures of Colby and Spinner

FR #	VG	VF	XF	AU	CU	CH-CU (63)	GEM (65)	S-GEM (66)	RARITY
1328spnmf	–	–	–	150	300	500	750	–	VERY SCARCE

Front with Wide Margins, with Autographed Signatures of Colby and Spinner

FR #	VG	VF	XF	AU	CU	CH-CU (63)	GEM (65)	S-GEM (66)	RARITY
1328spwmf	–	–	–	350	700	900	1200	–	VERY SCARCE

Front with Narrow Margins, with Autographed Signatures of Allison and Spinner

FR #	VG	VF	XF	AU	CU	CH-CU (63)	GEM (65)	S-GEM (66)	RARITY
1329spnmf	–	–	–	3000	4500	5900	–	–	RARE

Front with Wide Margins, with Autographed Signatures of Allison and Spinner

FR #	VG	VF	XF	AU	CU	CH-CU (63)	GEM (65)	S-GEM (66)	RARITY
1329spwmf	–	–	–	9000	14500	15900	–	–	VERY RARE 3 KNOWN

Proofs: Third Issue – Fifty Cent: Spinner

Fr. 1328spwmb, Back. Wide Margins

Fr. 1330aspwmb. Back. Wide Margins

Front with Narrow Margins, with Autographed Signatures of Jeffries and Spinner

FR #	VG	VF	XF	AU	CU	CH-CU (63)	GEM (65)	S-GEM (66)	RARITY
1330aspnmf	–	–	–	250	395	550	700	–	SCARCE

Front with Wide Margins, with Autographed Signatures of Jeffries and Spinner

FR #	VG	VF	XF	AU	CU	CH-CU (63)	GEM (65)	S-GEM (66)	RARITY
1330aspwmf	–	–	–	3500	7000	9000	–	–	VERY RARE 3 KNOWN

Green Back with Narrow Margins

FR #	VG	VF	XF	AU	CU	CH-CU (63)	GEM (65)	S-GEM (66)	RARITY
1331spnmb	–	–	–	100	125	250	395	–	COMMON

Green Back with Wide Margins

FR #	VG	VF	XF	AU	CU	CH-CU (63)	GEM (65)	S-GEM (66)	RARITY
1331spwmb	–	–	–	225	350	550	750	–	SCARCE

Red Back with Narrow Margins

FR #	VG	VF	XF	AU	CU	CH-CU (63)	GEM (65)	S-GEM (66)	RARITY
1328-30spnmb	–	–	–	175	250	395	495	–	SCARCE

Red Back with Wide Margins

FR #	VG	VF	XF	AU	CU	CH-CU (63)	GEM (65)	S-GEM (66)	RARITY
1328-30spwmb	–	–	–	350	450	750	1100	–	SCARCE VERY RARE IN GEM

Proofs: Third Issue – Fifty Cent: Spinner

Fr. 1331spwmb, Back. Wide Margins

Fr. 1339spwmb, Back. Wide Margins

Type 2, Green Back with Narrow Margins

FR #	VG	VF	XF	AU	CU	CH-CU (63)	GEM (65)	S-GEM (66)	RARITY
1339spnmb	–	–	–	3000	4500	5900	9000	–	VERY RARE 8 KNOWN

Type 2, Green Back with Wide Margins

FR #	VG	VF	XF	AU	CU	CH-CU (63)	GEM (65)	S-GEM (66)	RARITY
1339spwmb	–	–	–	4500	5500	7900	10000	–	VERY RARE 6-7 KNOWN

SIZE

Narrow Margins: 46-51 mm by 113-115 mm.

Wide Margins: 59-64 mm by 127-137 mm.

WIDE MARGIN BORDER *(Frame Line to Cutting Line)*

Front: 10 mm by 10 mm.

Back: 10 mm by 14 mm.

WHAT TO LOOK FOR

Check the autographed notes for "burn holes' (where the acid in the ink has burned through the thin paper). These notes are worth about half, or less, than the stated values.

NOTE: *Fr. 1330a spnmf and Fr. 1330a spwmf only come as Proofs.*

Proofs: Fourth Issue

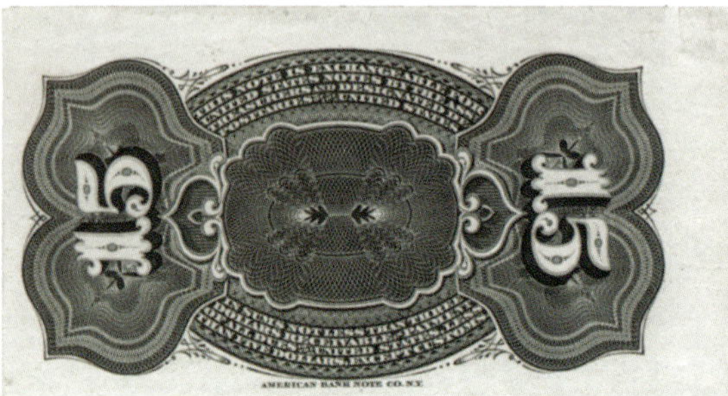

Fourth Issue Proofs

ISSUE	FACE	MILT #	VALUE (AU to GEM)
10¢	FRONT	4E10F.1	$900 – $1,600
10¢	BACK	4E10R.1	$500 – $1,200
15¢	FRONT	4E15F.1	$1,000 – $2,000
15¢	BACK	4E15R.1	$1,000 – $2,000
25¢	FRONT	4E25F.1	$1,200 – $3,000
25¢	BACK	4E25R.1	$500 – $1,200
50¢	FRONT	4E50F.1	$3,000 – $5,000
50¢	BACK	4E50R.1	$1,200 – $3,000

Proofs: Fifth Issue

MILT# 5E10R.2, Back

MILT# 5E25R.1, Back

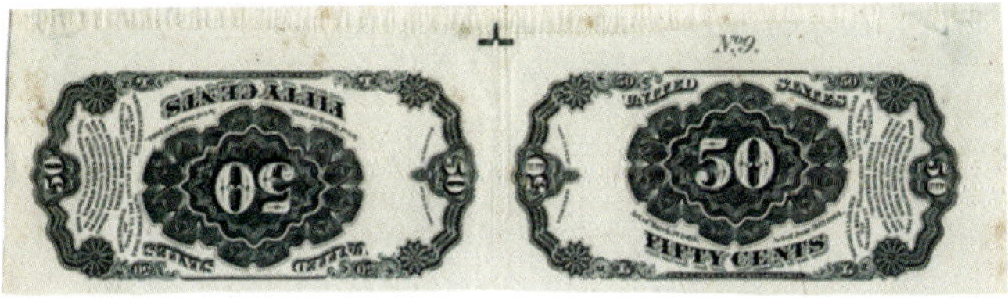

MILT# 5E50R.3, Back

Fifth Issue Proofs

ISSUE	FACE	MILT #	VALUE (AU to GEM)
10¢	FRONT	–	(None Known)
10¢	BACK	5E10R.2	$700 – $1,400
25¢	FRONT	–	(None Known)
25¢	BACK	5E25R.1	$900 – $1,800
50¢	FRONT	–	(None Known)
50¢	BACK	5E50R.3	$1,000 – $3,000

* Pricing is for single examples.

Part Five: Experimentals

V. EXPERIMENTALS

Experimental notes are basically just what their name implies. There are numerous varieties of Fractional Currency notes that were never issued. They experimented with different colors and formulas for ink. And, of course, there were many design ideas that were never released but small print runs were conducted to see what the notes looked like. These are very collectible.

Clark hired chemist and inventor, Dr. Stuart Gwynn, who developed the fiber paper notes of the second and third issues based upon these experiments. Many experiments on at least ten different kinds of paper were tried, mostly in second issue notes. Out of these experiments came the fiber paper notes of the second issue.

The experiments were tried to help stop the counterfeiting of Fractional Currency, as well as to try to save money on printing. Most of the experimental notes are cancelled with two half-moon holes. All of these are scarce to very scarce. Rarer still, are the ones cancelled with two or three pie-shaped holes. Very rare, and seldom seen, are the experimentals with no punch holes or cancellations. Since experimentals are a very specialized collection subset of Fractional Currency, I have only listed a few of the more common examples here.

For more detailed information, please refer to *The Encyclopedia of United States Fractional Currency*, by Milton R. Friedberg. Milt lists all of the various types of experimentals and has given them numbers from his system to help identify the different examples. The book is currently out of print, but they do turn up from time to time. It is possible to also get a re-print as a member of the Fractional Currency Collector's Board, a club devoted to the study and preservation of postage and fractional currency (see appendix).

Experimentals

2E5R.1a, Front

2E10F.4, Front

2E50F.4, Front

2E50R.3, Back

Second Issue – Five Cent

MILT #	DESCRIPTION	PRICE	RARITY
2E5R.1A	5¢, fiber paper front, Gem	$550.00	18-25 known

Second Issue – Ten Cent

MILT #	DESCRIPTION	PRICE	RARITY
2E10F.4	10¢, fiber paper front, ChCU	$500.00	20-30 known

Second Issue – Twenty-five Cent

MILT #	DESCRIPTION	PRICE	RARITY
2E50F.4	50¢, front, Gem	$750.00	15-20 known

Second Issue – Fifty Cent

MILT #	DESCRIPTION	PRICE	RARITY
2E50R.3	50¢, back, Gem	$750.00	15-20 known

Part Six: Fractional Currency Shields

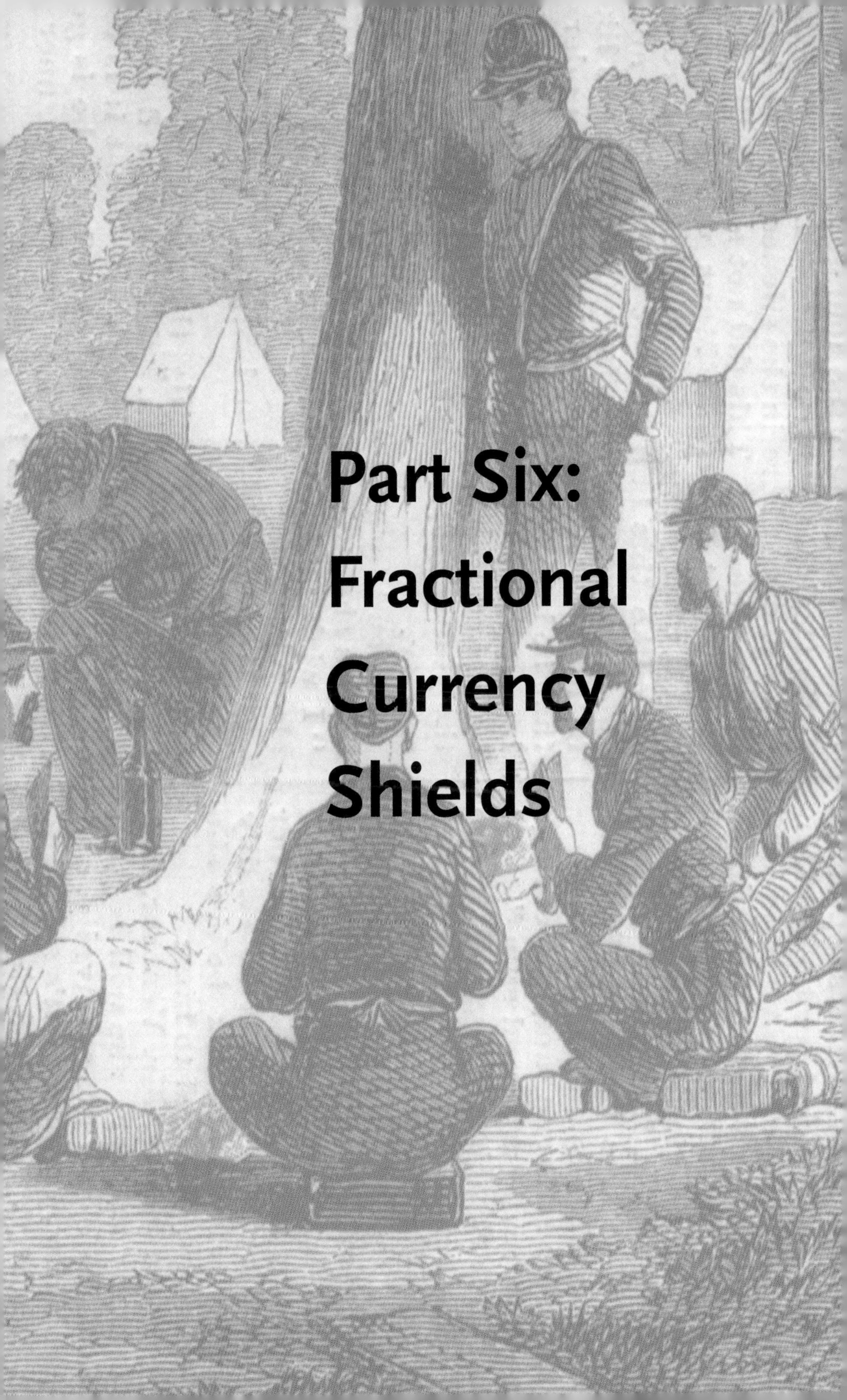

Fractional Currency Shields

Fractional currency shields were issued between June 1867 thru June of 1868. The plates for the 15¢ Grant/Sherman notes were not finished until May of 1867 and the shields have these notes, therefore the shields had to have been made after May of 1867. The plates for the type 2 50¢ Spinner backs were finished on June 24th of 1868 and these are not on any known shields. The absence of these suggest that the production of the shields had stopped by June of 1868.

In a letter from Treasurer Spinner, May 28th, 1868, he said that the shields were "sent free of express charges at $ 4.50 each." The total sales of shields was only $ 14,683.50, which means only 3,263 shields were sold! The demand for shields was not as good as was anticipated and many of the shields stored at the treasury were also water damaged. The remaining unsold shields were reportedly destroyed by the end of 1869.

A large shield was engraved on heavy paper. Above the shield is an arrangement of thirteen stars and an eagle on top. The shields are made up of 39 closely trimmed, narrow margin proofs. There are 20 fronts and 19 backs. They are from the first three issues and also the Grant/Sherman notes that were not issued.

Some say that the shields were made to assist bankers in identifying counterfeit fractional notes. If so, then why are the Grant/Sherman examples on the shields? Maybe they were just decorative Civil War souvenirs, since all three issues circulated during the Civil War! Since there are not very many pink and green shields, maybe they were made to give to some congressmen or others as special presentation versions.

Fractional Currency Shields

FR #	DESCRIPTION	VF	XF	AU	CU	CH-CU (63)	RARITY
1382	GRAY	2000	3000	4000	5K 6K	7K 9K	VERY SCARCE (est. 200-400)
1383	PINK	3000	7000	10000	14K 16K	18K 20K	RARE (est. 20-25)
1384	GREEN	9000	10000	18000	23K 30K	38K 50K	VERY RARE (est. 10-14)

SIZE

Cardboard Shields: 20 5/8" by 24-5/8".

WHAT TO LOOK FOR

Frames vary in size as the shields did not come framed from the government.

All shields display four notes with autographed signatures: 50¢ Justice, which is in the first row; 50¢ Spinner, in the second row; the 15¢ Grant/Sherman in the fourth row; and the 10¢ Washington in the sixth row. The green and pink shields (the earliest made) have Colby and Spinner autographs on all four hand-signed notes. The grey shields never have Colby and Spinner signatures on the Grant/Sherman examples.

Part Seven: Counterfeiting

Counterfeits and Counterfeiting

Fractional Currency collectors owe a debt to those arch criminals of the Civil War era who counterfeited Postage and Fractional currency notes. If it was not for the counterfeiters, the Government would not have found it necessary to print so many different notes, with so many varied issues and complex designs. The variety of these notes makes collecting more pleasurable and challenging.

WHAT TO LOOK FOR

Lathe work is very difficult to counterfeit. Genuine notes are made by a geometrical lathe. Counterfeits, for the most part, are made from hand-cut plates. On genuine work, the lathe work comes to small loops at the edges. Generally, counterfeited notes have no loops and are not as sharp and clear as the government-issued notes.

Human faces and vignettes on genuine notes are vital and lifelike. These same elements on counterfeited notes are mostly blurred and expressionless, the eyes full, the hair imperfect and so forth. The differences are obvious once the collector sees a real side-by side comparison.

Counterfeit notes are sometimes missing "flourishes." Flourishes are engraved lines used to enhance the design of original and authentic notes. Fake notes may also include misspelled words and will frequently use the wrong letters or numbers for surcharges. One example being the counterfeit Fr. 1373A, which has an "8" when it should display an "S" in the reverse surcharge.

Illustration from "Heath's Infallible Counterfeit Detector", 1870, of an Fr. 1324. The bottom note is the forgery. Note the missing flourish line from the top right corner, and the lack of sharpness in the eyes of the subject, the differences in the quality of the hair lines and mustache.

Part Eight: Presentation Books

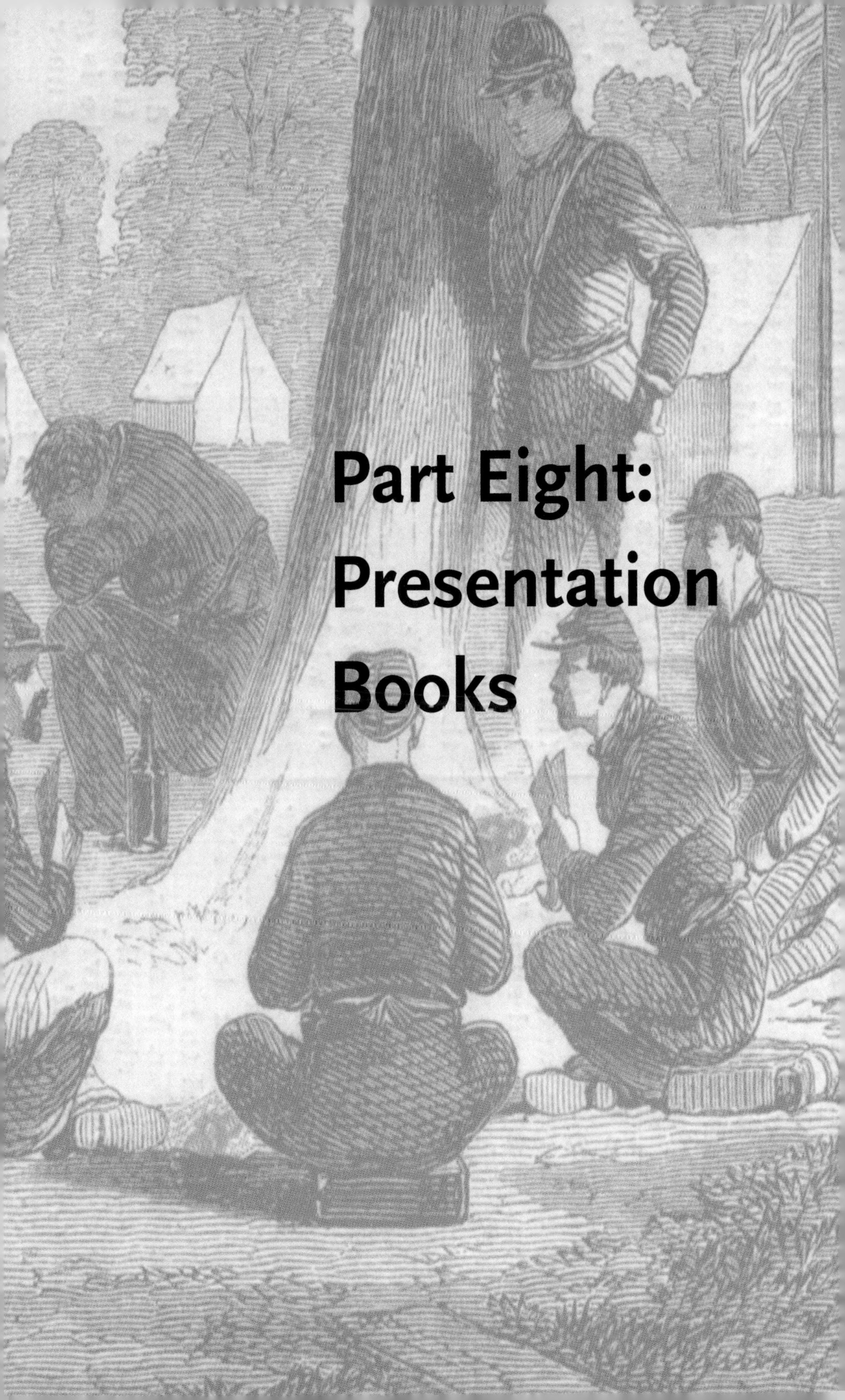

Fractional Currency Presentation Books

Fractional Currency Presentation Books

One of the most historic and rarest of Fractional Currency items are the Presentation books. They were presented to President Andrew Johnson and his cabinet and a few congressmen, on May 9th and 10th, 1866. Of the 18 books made, three are in museums and the location or status of another seven is unknown. Therefore, this leaves only eight collectable Presentation Books at this time.

They are small books, 43/4 x 63/8 inches, gold stamped, leather bound. The covers have ornate scrollwork and most of the books have a personalized front cover with the recipient's name and title gold embossed on the cover.

All the books contain the same 31 proof notes, with vivid impressions. All are uniface with no bronzing overprints. Twenty four of these proof notes are found only in these presentation books. The last one sold to a collector for $27,000.00.

PRESENTATION BOOK PROVENANCE

Originally presented to (followed by subsequent owners):

1. **President Andrew Johnson**
    - William Philpot
    - B. Max Mehl
    - Milt Friedberg
    - Martin Gengerke
    - Douglas Hale
    - Thomas O'Mara
    - (Unknown)

2. **Salmon P. Chase,** Chief Justice of the Supreme Court
    (Current whereabouts unknown.)

3. **F. E. Spinner, Treasurer**
    - George Slawson
    - Robert Russel
    - Dr. Ronald Kessler
    - Martin Gengerke
    - Milton Friedberg
    - Howard Cohen (Current owner)

4. **William H. Seward,** Secretary of State
    (Current whereabouts unknown.)

5. **Edwin M. Stanton,** Secretary of War
    (Current whereabouts unknown.)

6. **Gideon Wells,** Secretary of the Navy
    - Wells Family
    - Martin Gengerke
    - Herman Halpern
    - Currently with a Long Island, NY., Collector

Fractional Currency Presentation Books

7. **Hugh McCulloch,** Secretary of the Treasury
   (Current whereabouts unknown.)

8. **James Harlan,** Secretary of the Interior
   (Current whereabouts unknown.)

9. **James Speed,** Attorney General
   (Current whereabouts unknown.)

10. **William Dennison,** Postmaster General
    - Robert Herdegen
    - A.N.A. Museum (Current)

11. **L. S. Foster,** President Pro Tem of the Senate
    - B. Max Mehl
    - Wayne Raymond
    - Herman Crofoot
    - Smithsonian Institution (Current)

12. **Senator William P. Fessenden**
    - Fessenden Family
    - A.N.S. Museum (Current)

13. **Schuyler Colfax,** Speaker of the House
    (Current whereabouts unknown)

14. **Spencer M. Clark**, Superintendent of the National Currency Bureau
    - Dr. E. R. Hodge
    - Col. E. H. R. Green
    - F.C.C. Boyd
    - John J. Ford, Jr.
    - (Unknown)

15. **Spencer M. Clark,** Superintendent of the National Currency Bureau
    - Stack's
    - Herman Halpern
    - (Unknown)

16. **William C. Chandler,** Assistant Secretary of the Treasury
    - Tom Denly
    - Martin Gengerke
    - Dr. H. A. Scheuerman
    - Currently with a Long Island, NY., Collector

17. **Unknown Recipient**
    - F. G. Kirchner
    - Robert Kravitz
    - Currently with a California Collector

18. **Unknown Recipient**
    - Douglas Hales
    - (Unknown)

Part Nine: Original Bundles

Original Bundles

WHAT TO LOOK FOR

In original bundles, all notes should have square edges with no notes sticking out. The wave and paper texture should be the same on all notes.

As a protection against theft, most original bundles will have a needle hole in the upper right-hand corner where the notes were stitched together. If only a few of the notes in a bundle have this needle hole the bundle was put together and is not an original bundle. Bundle bands are sometimes sold separately for approximately $50.00 each at current rates.

Original Bundles

Issue	FR #	CU	CH-CU (63)	GEM (65)	RARITY	DESCRIPTION
4th Issue						
10¢	1259		7500	10000	Only 2 Known	50 Notes
50¢	1379	3600	4800	8500	Less than 20 Known	20 Notes
5th Issue						
10¢	1265		5000			50 Notes Long Thin Key
10¢	1266	3000	5000	9000		50 Notes
25¢	1309	3300	5700	8000		40 Notes
50¢	1381	3200	4100	7000		20 Notes

Part Ten: Sheets

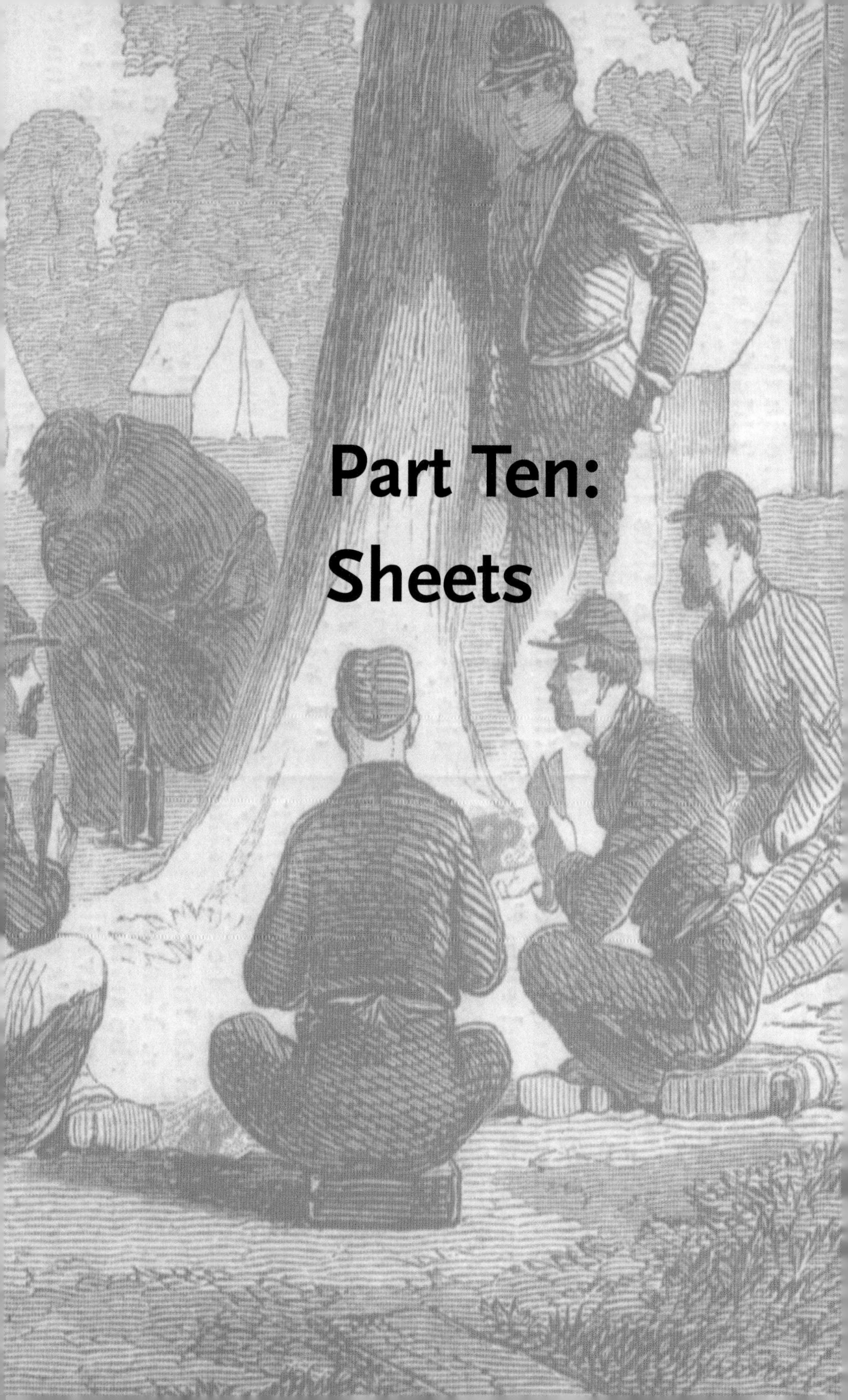

Sheets

SHEET PLATE NUMBER LOCATIONS

1st Issue - 5¢, 10¢, 25¢ & 50¢

The plate numbers appear on the untrimmed left edge of the sheet, both front and back.

2nd Issue - 5¢, 10¢, 25¢ & 50¢

Plate numbers appear at the intersection of the square of the four notes at the lower left corner of the sheet.

3rd Issue

Plate numbers appear at the intersection of the four notes in the lower left corner both front and back of sheet.

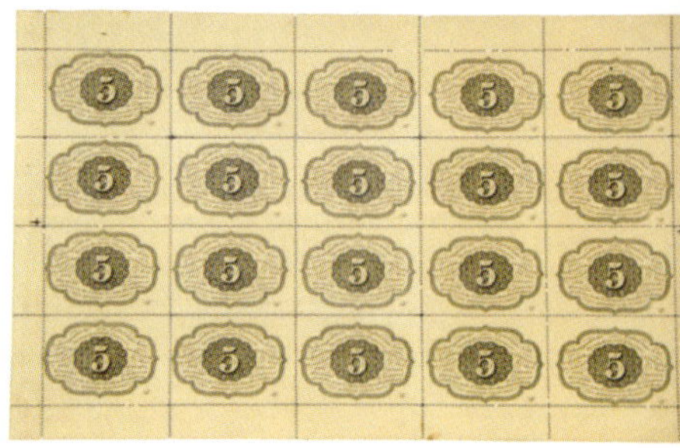

SEAL PLATE NUMBER LOCATIONS

4th Issue

Seal plate numbers are at the intersection of both the four lower left and four lower-right notes of the sheet. See Appendix VIII.

Sheets

Issue	FR #	XF	AU	CU	CH-CU (63)	GEM (65)	Description
st Issue							
5¢	1230		2600	3200	4000	5000	Full Sheet = 20 Notes
10¢	1242		3900	4500	5000	5900	Full Sheet = 20 Notes
25¢	1281		3900	4500	5000	6500	Full Sheet = 16 Notes
50¢	1312		4300	5000	7000	12000	Full Sheet = 16 Notes, Only 9 – 10 Known
nd Issue							
5¢	1232		2800	3200	3500	4100	Full Sheet = 20 Notes
10¢	1244		3000	3400	3700	4300	Full Sheet = 20 Notes
25¢	1283		3200	3600	3900	4600	Full Sheet = 20 Notes
50¢	1316		3800	4500	5000	6500	Full Sheet = 20 Notes
rd Issue							
3¢	1226	2500	3000	4500	7000	9000	Full Sheet = 25 Notes
	1227	11000					Full Sheet = 25 Notes, Only 3 Known
	1227		2000				Block of 6

WHAT TO LOOK FOR

Buy sheets with the selvage border of the sheet still there. Some sheets are trimmed down to the notes to remove a corner fold or other imperfections.

Perforated sheets are known, but extremely rare, with only a few of each known.

Less than 5 known of the Fr. 1228 perforated sheets with the last one selling at $ 9,200.00 in 2006.

Less than 5 known of the Fr. 1240 perforated sheets with the last sale at $14,000.00 in 2006.

Of the 3 known Fr. 1279, the last one to sell was in 2006 and fetched $16,100.00

There are 3 known Fr. 1310 sheets, with the last one sold for $18,400.00 in 2006 as well.

Sheets

	NOTE	FRONT PLATE NUMBERS OBSERVED	BACK PLATE NUMBERS OBSERVED
First Issue*			
	5¢	1,18,21,25,35,36,48	15,35,47
	10¢	5,6,20,33	12,30,31
	25¢	1,5,10	9
	50¢	5,10,20,26	20,22
Second Issue**			
	5¢		
	10¢		–
	25¢		–
	50¢		–
Third Issue***			
	3¢	Fr. 1226:	20
		Fr. 1227:	67
	5¢	19	1
	10¢	26	4
	25¢		
	50¢ Justice		
	50¢ Spinner		

* Because plate numbers appear on the left and right selvage that is usually trimmed off, plate numbers on first issue notes is very rare.

Less than 5 5¢ perforated sheets known. Fr. 1228 sold for $9,200.00 on 3/7/2000

Less than 5 10¢ perforated sheets known. Fr. 1240 sold for $11,500.00 on 3/7/2006 then for $14,000.00 on 4/1/2006.

Just 3 or 4 of the 25¢ perforated sheets known. Fr. 1279 sold for $16,000.00 on 3/7/2006.

**Only 2 or 3 perforated sheets known. Fr. 1310 sold for $18,400.00 on 3/7/2006.

*** The dark back ground Fr. 1227 were made from just 7 face plates while the light back ground Fr. 1226's were made from 33 different face plates.

The only known red back full sheet of 5¢ 3rd Issue notes contains 16 Fr. 1236 and 4 Fr. 1237 notes, with face plate 19 and back plate 1, sold for $37,600.00 on 5/11/2004.

A unique red back full sheet of 16 notes, containing 12 Fr. 1251 and 4 Fr. 1252 with face plate 26 and back plate 4 sold for $20,700.00 on 5/11/2004.

Part Eleven: Errors

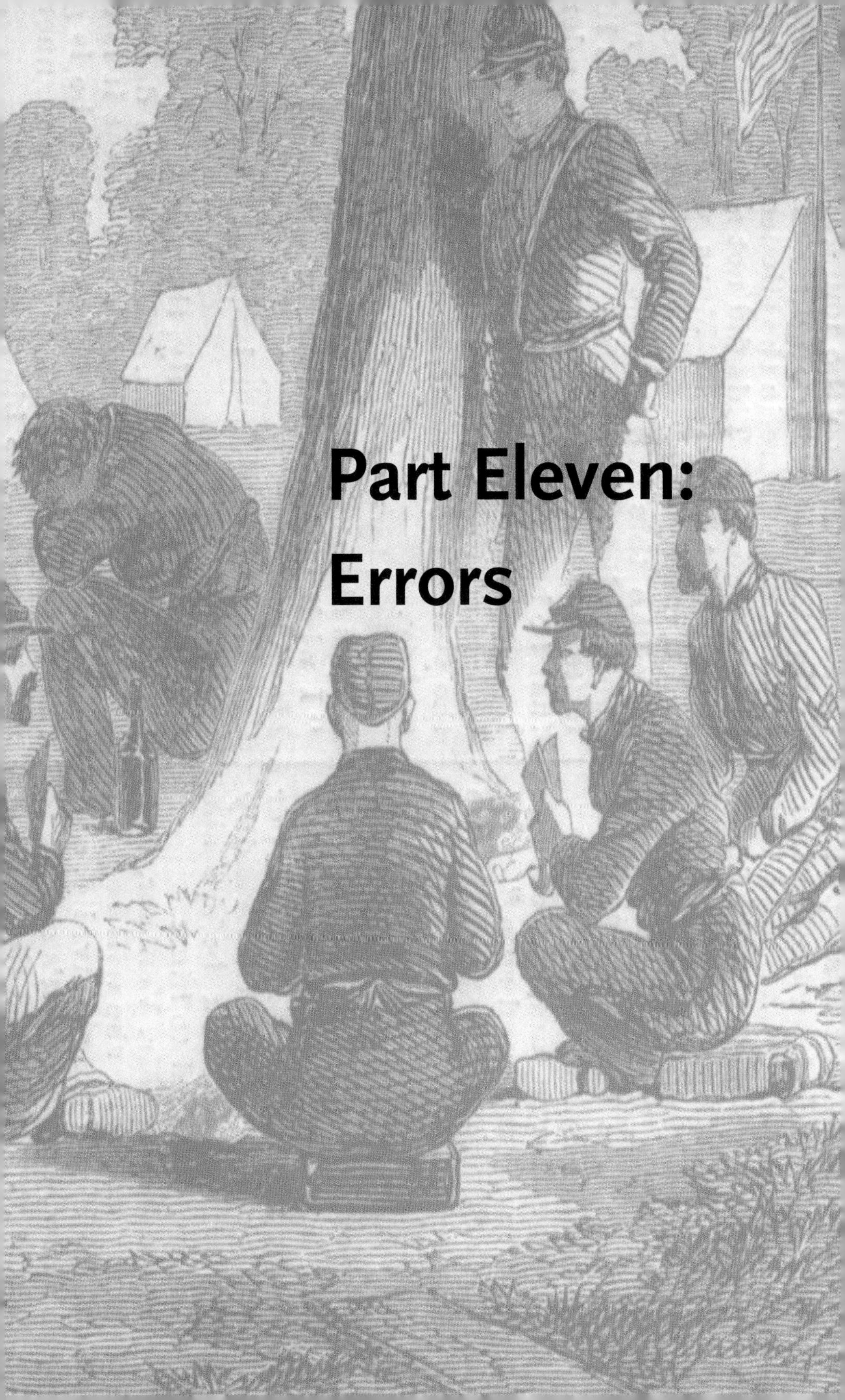

Errors

Errors can be made during any printing process. Fractional currency errors seem to be less numerous than other paper money errors and, while a few are common, most are rare. Prices for Fractional Currency notes with errors vary considerably. Anywhere from $20.00 up to thousands of dollars can be seen. Check with your favorite Fractional Currency dealer before you sell or buy.

For more detailed information, please refer to "Fractional Currency Errors," by Benny Bolin in *Paper Money*, Vol. XLII, No. 1. The magazine issued by the Society of Paper money Collectors.

Here are some things to look for:

Double denomination errors: Here, the front and back are printed from different notes, e.g. a 10¢ front and a 50¢ back. These are very rare with less than ten known. Be wary of fiber paper double denomination notes as these can be easily made by marrying two different easily separated notes.

Misalignment: The most common Fractional Currency error. Here one side of the note, usually the front, is well centered while the back is off center. Some have just a little of the next note, and some have a large part of the adjacent note showing. Look for notes where about half of the next design is showing. Notes with just a part of the next note showing are less valuable.

Inverts: The most collected Fractional Currency error. Some "Inverts" have inverted back design in relation to the front. Others have inverted surcharges. Some appear with just the design inverted, most of these are second and third issue notes. Bronzing errors also appear in various forms. Some are misaligned and some are missing. Blurred bronze surcharges are not errors. This is more like a smear that occurs when too much bronze is applied. Beware of 50¢, second issue notes with no surcharges, as there are no genuine notes known.

Gutter fold errors: This happens when a sheet has a wrinkle at the time of printing. Then, after the notes are printed the wrinkle may flatten out leaving a streak of non-printed paper. These errors are somewhat common on small size currency, but are very rare on larger denomination notes. (Shown at right.)

Errors

Missing Seal: There are between five and ten fourth and fifth issue notes with no seal, that are considered to be genuine. Most that I've seen have had the seals scraped, erased or chemically removed.

Appendix

Appendix I – Hidden Treasure

HOW TO FIND BARGINS

Believe it or not, coin shows are the best place to find Fractional Currency bargains. Coin dealers and paper currency dealers use different techniques to determine value and rarity. If you see Fractional Currency at a coin show or dealer's shop, stop and take a look. Even if a note looks bad on first inspection, it could be a treasure if you do your homework. Most coin dealers set their prices by the well known trader guide called the "Greensheet." This publication often mixes rare and valuable numbers with more common notes. Some coin dealers overlook the more desirable Fractionals and price them accordingly. Mistakes in type, number and grade can lead to a bargain for you.

Here are a few examples:

Some antique stores specialize in Civil War collectibles. Items like water canteens and paper wrapped bullets are common. Some of these dealers have currency on display and the dealers rarely know what's what. You can frequently see all types of currency lumped together with coins and postage stamps on postcards and old letters. In some states you can see Confederate currency lumped together with Union Fractional notes. If you know the ins and outs of these notes you can "pick" a sleeper. Even a simple AU condition note can be worth ten times what the dealer is asking.

Another example comes from visiting coin shows, even some stamp shows will prove profitable. At a recent coin show in St. Louis, a sharp eyed currency dealer spotted a sleeper in a coin dealers display case. This was a Justice note showing a "1" and an "a" as position indicators. The note was marked Fr. 1360 and had a relative low price attached. But, a note with these two position markers might easily be more valuable. I repeat, do your homework. This is why I brought out this book with price and rarity guides. The note was in great shape and turned out to be a rare Fr. 1359, and although it wasn't in GEM condition (in fact, it was only AU) the note was so rare it still fetched $1,800.00 at auction, less than one year later. That's a five-fold return on a $350.00 investment. You do the math.

In another example, a fractional collector, looking through notes at a coin dealer's case came across a note marked Fr. 1298, but since it had front, solid surcharges, the collector recognized it as a very scarce Fr. 1299. He couldn't get the money out of his wallet fast enough. He paid less than $100.00 for that note, worth $1,200.00 on an average day.

In my final example, another fractional collector was looking at albums a stamp dealer had at a recent show. One of the albums contained some fractional currency, as it's not uncommon for stamp dealers to have some examples, especially of the perforated first-issue notes. The collector came upon a circulated 2nd issue 25¢ note with a dark, gray back. He quickly paid the dealer the $75.00asking price and walked away with a rare, slate-back Fr. 1286a worth almost 5 times the price paid to the stamp dealer.

TURNING PAPER INTO GOLD

I have included a list of major coin and currency shows in the appendix in this book, but not all of the big Fractional Currency collectors or shows are located in the Northeast. Two of the top ten collectors in the country live in the west. I can not reveal the city or state for security reasons, but ironically these collectors live less than ten miles from each other. Even more ironically, they have never met. One of the collectors has a complete collection of regular issue notes and the only possible complete collection of narrow and wide margin specimen notes. The other collector is only four or five notes away from a complete set of regular issue notes and very close to a complete set of specimen notes. One of them is one of only three or four people to own all three shields (gray, pink and green) and a Presentation Book at the same time. Another collector on the east side of the country holds a complete regular issue collection. I would estimate each collection could easily be worth anywhere from $500,000 to over a million dollars.

So keep searching, you never know what you'll discover!

Appendix II – Type Sets

1st ISSUE	VALUE	DESCRIPTION
Fr. 1230	5¢	Straight Edges
Fr. 1242	10¢	Straight Edges
Fr. 1281	25¢	Straight Edges
Fr. 1312	50¢	Straight Edges
2nd ISSUE		
Fr. 1232	5¢	Without Surcharges
Fr. 1244	10¢	Without Surcharges
Fr. 1283	25¢	Without Surcharges
Fr. 1317	50¢	Surcharge "A-18-63" OR
Fr. 1318	50¢	Surcharge "1-18-63"
3rd ISSUE		
Fr. 1226	3¢	Light Background
Fr. 1238	5¢	Clark Green Back
Fr. 1255	10¢	Green Back
Fr. 1294	25¢	Green Back
Fr. 1331	50¢	Spinner Green Back
Fr. 1358	50¢	Justice Green Back
4th ISSUE		
Fr. 1257	10¢	Liberty
Fr. 1267	15¢	Columbia
Fr. 1301	25¢	Washington
Fr. 1374	50¢	Lincoln
Fr. 1376	50¢	Stanton
Fr. 1379	50¢	Dexter
5th ISSUE		
Fr. 1265	10¢	Meredith
Fr. 1308	25¢	Walker
Fr. 1381	50¢	Crawford
Grant/Sherman		
Fr. 1272sp	15¢	Narrow Margin Front
Fr. 1272sp	15¢	Narrow Margin Front Green Back

Appendix II – Type Sets

1st ISSUE	VALUE	DESCRIPTION
Fr. 1228 or Fr. 1229	5¢	Perforated Edges
Fr. 1230 or Fr. 1231	5¢	Straight Edges
Fr. 1240 or Fr. 1241	10¢	Perforated Edges
Fr. 1242 or Fr. 1243	10¢	Straight Edges
Fr. 1279 or Fr. 1280	25¢	Perforated Edges
Fr. 1281 or Fr. 1282	25¢	Straight Edges
Fr. 1310 or Fr. 1311	50¢	Perforated Edges
Fr. 1312 or Fr. 1313	50¢	Straight Edges
2nd ISSUE		
Fr. 1232 - Fr. 1234	5¢	
Fr. 1235	5¢	Fiber Paper
Fr. 1244 - Fr. 1248	10¢	
Fr. 1249	10¢	Fiber Paper
Fr. 1283 - Fr. 1288	25¢	
Fr. 1289 or Fr. 1290 2	5¢	Fiber Paper
Fr. 1314 - Fr. 1318	50¢	
Fr. 1320 - Fr. 1322	50¢	Fiber Paper
Fr. 1226	3¢	Light Background
Fr. 1227	3¢	Dark Background
Fr. 1236 or Fr. 1237	5¢	Red Back
Fr. 1238 or Fr. 1239	5¢	Green Back
Fr. 1252 or Fr. 1252	10¢	Red Back
Fr. 1253 or Fr. 1254	10¢	Red Back - Autographed
Fr. 1255 or Fr. 1256	10¢	Green Back
Fr. 1291 or Fr. 1292	25¢	Red Back
Fr. 1294 - Fr. 1296	25¢	Green Back
Fr. 1297 - Fr. 1300	25¢	Fiber Paper
Fr. 1324 - Fr. 1327	50¢	Spinner Red Back
3rd ISSUE		
Fr. 1328 - Fr. 1330	50¢	Spinner Red Back - Autographed
Fr. 1331 - Fr. 1338	50¢	Spinner Green Back - Type 1 Back
Fr. 1339 - Fr. 1342	50¢	Spinner Green Back - Type 2 Back
Fr. 1343 - Fr. 1350	50¢	Justice Red Back
Fr. 1357	50¢	Justice Red BackFiber Paper
Fr. 1355 or Fr. 1356	50¢	Justice Red Back - Autographed
Fr. 1358 - Fr. 1369	50¢	Justice Green Back
Fr. 1370 - Fr. 1373	50¢	Justice Green Back - Fiber Paper

Appendix II – Type Sets

4th ISSUE	VALUE	DESCRIPTION
Fr. 1257 - Fr. 1261	10¢	
Fr. 1267 - Fr. 1271	15¢	
Fr. 1301 - Fr. 1307	25¢	
Fr. 1374	50¢	Lincoln
Fr. 1376	50¢	Stanton
Fr. 1379	50¢	Dexter
5th ISSUE		
Fr. 1264	10¢	Green Seal
Fr. 1265 - Fr. 1266	10¢	Red Seal
Fr. 1308 or Fr. 1309	25¢	
Fr. 1381	50¢	Crawford

GRANT/SHERMAN 15¢ NOTES

NOTE	DESCRIPTION
Fr. 1272 spnmf	Face, Narrow Margin, Printed Signatures
Fr. 1272 spnmb	Green Back, Narrow Margin
Fr. 1273 spnmf	Face, Narrow Margin, Autograph Signatures of Colby & Spinner
Fr. 1274 spnmf	Face, Narrow Margin, Autograph Signatures of Jeffries & Spinner
Fr. 1275 spnmf	Face, Narrow Margin, Autograph Signatures of Allison & Spinner
Fr. 1273 - Fr. 1275spnmb	Red Back, Narrow Margin
Fr. 1272 spwmf	Face, Wide Margin, Printed Signatures
Fr. 1274 spwmf	Face, Wide Margin, Autographed Signatures of Jeffries & Spinner
Fr. 1275 spwmf	Face, Wide Margin, Autographed Signatures of Allison & Spinner
Fr. 1272 spwmb	Green Back, Wide Margin
Fr. 1273 - Fr. 1275spwmb	Red Back, Wide Margin

How Many Grant/Sherman Notes are Left?

My Estimate, What do You Think?

As of 1884 only 3,513 pairs of all types of Grant/Sherman notes were still outstanding (printed and autographed signatures, narrow and wide margins, fronts and backs). How many have been lost, burned in fires, or turned-in over the past 125 years? So that brings us to 2011, just reduce that number by only 50%, which comes to 1,756 pairs of all types remaining.

How many are still left on shields? There are two fronts and two backs on each shield and there are maybe 450 shields still left! So there is 1,756 - 900 = 856. So I estimate there may be 600 to 800 left. Wide margins are two times as scarce as the narrow margins. So whether wide or narrow, I think the following is true:

- Fr. 1274's - Are two times as scarce as Fr. 1272's.
- Fr. 1275's - Are two times as scarce as Fr. 1274's.
- Red Backs are two times as scarce as the Green Backs

The following are my estimates of how many are left:

Fronts:

Note	Narrow	Wide
Fr. 1272	200	100
Fr. 1273	57	(Unknown)
Fr. 1274	100	50
Fr. 1275	50	25

Backs:

Note	Narrow	Wide
Green	240	120
Red	120	50

Appendix V – Fractional Inverts

1st ISSUE - INVERTED - BACK ONLY

	NOTE	KNOWN CENSUS
5¢	Fr. 1228	1
	Fr. 1229	1
	Fr. 1230	35+
	Fr. 1331	1 AU
10¢	Fr. 1240 (None Known)	
	Fr. 1241	2 (F & XF)
	Fr. 1242	20+
	Fr. 1243	4 (1 CHCU)
25¢	Fr. 1279	(None Known)
	Fr. 1280	5
	Fr. 1281	12 (1 AU+, 4 CU)
	Fr. 1282	10
50¢	Fr. 1310	1
	Fr. 1311	1
	Fr. 1312	6 (1 CHCU)
	Fr. 1313	2 (1 AU)

Appendix V – Fractional Inverts

2nd ISSUE - INVERTED NOTES

	NOTE	INVERTED ENGRAVING	INVERTED SURCHARGE	TOTAL BACK
5¢	Fr. 1232		3	35+
	Fr. 1233	1 (GEM)	8	1
	Fr. 1234-Fr. 1335		(None Known)	
10¢	Fr. 1244		2	
	Fr. 1245		10	
	Fr. 1246	4	20+	1
	Fr. 1247		2	
	Fr. 1248		None Known)	
	Fr. 1249		2	
25¢	Fr. 1283		5	
	Fr. 1284	1	1	
	Fr. 1285			
	Fr. 1286	3	4	
	Fr. 1288		1	
	Fr. 1289		1	
	Fr. 1290		1 (VF)	
50¢	Fr. 1316		1	
	Fr. 1317	1 (CU)	2 (VG, VF+)	
	Fr. 1318		3 (1 GEM)	2
	Fr. 1320 (		None Known)	
	Fr. 1321			1
	Fr. 1322	1	1	1 (AU)

Appendix V – Fractional Inverts

3rd ISSUE - INVERTED NOTES

	NOTE	INVERTED ENGRAVING	INVERTED SURCHARGE	TOTAL BACK
3¢	Fr. 1226	6	N/A	N/A
	Fr. 1227	1 (F+)	N/A	N/A
5¢	Fr. 1236-Fr. 1237	(None Known)	N/A	N/A
	Fr. 1238 7	(1 GEM)	N/A	N/A
	Fr. 1339	3	N/A	N/A
10¢	Fr. 1251- Fr. 1254	(None Known)	N/A	N/A
	Fr. 1255	1 (CHCU)	4 Face Surcharges 4 Back & Face Surcharges	
	Fr. 1256		1 (VF)	
25¢	Fr. 1291		2 Back Surcharges	
	Fr. 1292		(None Known)	
	Fr. 1294	1	10-12 Back Surcharges	
	Fr. 1295	1	2 Back	
			Surcharges	
	Fr. 1296		(None Known)	
	Fr. 1297		1 Back Surcharges	
	Fr. 1298	3 (1 CU)		
	Fr. 1299		1 (XF)	
	Fr. 1300		(None Known)	
50¢	Fr. 1224- Fr. 1330		(None Known)	
	Fr. 1331	1	1	1
	Fr. 1332		3	1
	Fr. 1333	1	1	1
	Fr. 1334	1	1	1
	Fr. 1335	1	4	1
	Fr. 1336	1	1	
	Fr. 1337	1	1 (VF)	
	Fr. 1338	1	2 (1AU)	
	Fr. 1339		2	1 (XF)
	Fr. 1340		1	
	Fr. 1341		2	
	Fr. 1342		1	
	Fr. 1343-Fr. 1356		(None Known)	
	Fr. 1357		10	
	Fr. 1358-Fr. 1359		(None Known)	

Appendix V – Fractional Inverts

3rd ISSUE - INVERTED NOTES (Cont.)

	NOTE	INVERTED ENGRAVING	INVERTED SURCHARGE	TOTAL BACK
50¢	Fr. 1360		1	
	Fr. 1361		(None Known)	
	Fr. 1362	1	3	
	Fr. 1363		1	
	Fr. 1364		3-4	
	Fr. 1365		3	1
	Fr. 1366		5	
	Fr. 1367		1	
	Fr. 1368		1	
	Fr. 1369		1	
	Fr. 1370	3	3	1
	Fr. 1371	1	1	
	Fr. 1372	1	1	
	Fr. 1373	2	3	
	Fr. 1373a		(None Known)	

The use of the tête-bêche (French for "head-to-tail") technique of laying-out engraving plates was the end of inverts caused by printing errors. This was used beginning on the 5th issue notes. The following example illustrates:

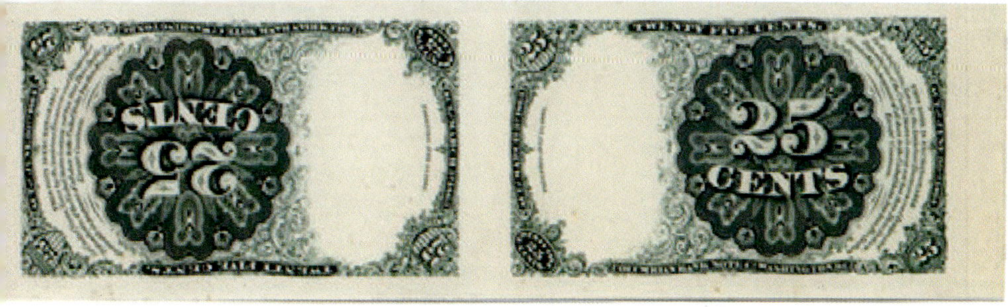

Appendix VI – Tim Prusmack: "Mozart Of Money"

A MEMORIAL TRIBUTE TO THE "MOZART OF MONEY"

TIM PRUSMACK (1962 - 2004)

I collect Rock'n'Roll posters from the 1960's & 1970's. One of the best poster artists is Stanley Mouse. I once showed him some of Tim Prusmacks fractional notes (Lincoln & Spinner) next to the real notes and he said "the man is a great artist, I'm sure glad he was not around here (San Francisco) in the 60's!"

Just like Stanley Mouse, Tim excelled in reproducing, by hand, his artistic money. He did many large size, small size and fractional notes, and all are great works of art. A lasting testimonial to the "Mozart of Money" - Tim Prusmack. He was always friendly and kind to everyone who came up to his table, whether they bought something or not.

In Memphis, 2002, Tim came out with his Grant/Sherman notes, both in wide and narrow margins. They were truly amazing! He had made only 125 signed and numbered of each, and one promotional note that was 48" by 28". I just had to have the large promotional note since Grant/Sherman's are my favorite notes!

It was not for sale! Tim said he needed it to promote the notes that he had. So I said if I buy the rest of his notes, can I buy the big Grant/Sherman? "But I have a lot left" he said. I ended-up buying all but 10 of each, which he kept for the rest of the show. I now own the largest Grant/Sherman note ever made! Thank-you Tim!

Appendix VII – Dates of Postage and Fractional Currency Production

Postage and Fractional Currency Dates of Production*

	NOTES	DESCRIPTION	NUMBER PRODUCED	PRODUCTION DATE
First Issue				
	–	Straight Edges with No Monogram	–	A Few Weeks Beginning August 21st, 1862
	–	Perforated Edges with No Monogram	–	Next Few Weeks into September, 1862
	–	Perforated Edges with ABNCo Monogram	–	Latter Part of September and Early October, 1862
	–	Straight Edges with ABNCo Monogram	–	December, 1862 to May 27th, 1863
	–	All First Issue Production	–	August 21st, 1862 to May 27th, 1863
Second Issue				
	Fiber Paper Notes	All Second Issue Fiber Paper Notes:	–	October 10th, 1863 to October 1st, 1864
	5¢	Fr. 1235	11,837	–
	10¢	Fr. 1249	17,098	–
	25¢	Fr. 1289 & Fr. 1290	58,689	–
	50¢	Fr. 1320, Fr. 1321 & Fr. 1322	62,300	–
	–	All Remaining Second Issue Notes	–	November, 1864 to March, 1865
Third Issue				
	3¢	Fr. 1226 & Fr. 1227	–	January 23rd to April 5th 1865
	5¢	–	–	January, 1865 to April, 1866
	10¢			
		Fr. 1251	18,000	August 26th to September 19th, 1865
	Fr. 1253	–	–	June, 1866 to October, 1867
	Fr. 1254	–	–	October, 1867 through November, 1867
		Green Backs	–	December, 1867 Through April, 1869
	15¢	Grant/Sherman Pairs	9,016	May, 1867
	25¢			
		Red Back Notes - Fr. 1291 & Fr. 1292	16,000	February 21st through March 6th, 1865
		Fiber Paper - Fr. 1297, Fr. 1298, Fr. 1299 & Fr. 1300	7,107	March 22, 1865
		All Green Back Notes	-	April, 1865 to April, 1869

Appendix VII – Dates of Postage and Fractional Currency Production

	NOTES	DESCRIPTION	NUMBER PRODUCED	PRODUCTION DATE
	50¢			
		Fr. 1357	3,060	December 5th, 1864
		Red Back Justice Notes	–	January 14th, 1865 to February, 1865
		Green Back Justice Notes	–	February, 1865 to December, 1865
		Spinner with Type-1 Backs	–	January 1st, 1866 to March 23rd, 1868
		Spinner with Type-2 Backs	–	May 27th, 1868 to April 15th, 1869
Fourth Issue				
	Note: Notes of All Denominations Produced from July through December, 1869 were Watermarked "**USUSUSUSUSUS**"			
	10¢			
		Large Seal Variety Fr. 1257, Fr. 1258 & Fr. 1259	179,097,000	July 14th, 1869 to December, 1871
		Small Seal Variety Fr. 1261	170,32,600	January, 1872 to February, 1875
	15¢			
		Large Seal Variety Fr. 1267, Fr. 1268 & Fr. 1269	27,240,040	July, 1869 to December, 1871
		Small Seal Variety Fr. 1271	8,121,400	April, 1872 to March 1874
	25¢			
		Large Seal Variety Fr. 1301, Fr. 1302 & Fr. 1303	–	July, 1869 to December 1869
		Small Seal Variety Fr. 1307	–	January, 1872 to February, 1874
	50¢ Lincoln	–	–	December, 1869
	50¢ Stanton	–	–	January, 1870 to June, 1873
	50¢ Dexter	–	–	August 3rd, 1873 to February 16th, 1874
Fifth Issue	10¢, 25¢ & 50¢	All Notes	–	July, 1874 to February, 1876

* This data supplied by Walter Breen.

Appendix VIII – Fractional Currency Plate Numbers

FRACTIONAL PLATE NUMBERS

by Rick Melamed

In order to print fractional currency, the Treasury used engraved steel plates for its production. Since millions of notes were produced, hundreds of plates were required as plates wore out over time. In order for the Treasury to keep track, plates were engraved with plate numbers. Often the plate numbers were in the actual body of the sheet (in the 2nd, 3rd and 4th issues); so when the sheet was cut into individual notes, plate numbers would appear. They were strictly used for accounting purposes and not part of the design. The result is plate numbers appear in various forms and designs. It is interesting to note that while the actual subject plates were etched in exacting detail, the actual plate numbers had no set design. Hence we see a range from plain numerals to the rococo design with curlicues and other embellishments.

There are 2 kinds of plate numbers used on fractional currency. The first is sheet plate numbers and the second is seal plate numbers. And within these 2 groups, there are quite a few plate numbers engraved inverted (upside down) or in mirror image.

Sheet Plate Numbers

Fractional notes were printed in sheets from 8 to as many as 50 subjects. To track the plates used, numerals were engraved into the actual subject plate of all fractionals. These are known as sheet plate numbers. Different issues have different use of plate numbers and there is no consistent numbering pattern on fractional notes.

First Issue. In the first issue, sheet plate numbers were engraved in the selvage and would only appear if the note was untrimmed. Plate numbers never appear in the body of the note. Shown below is an FR1310 with the perforated selvage attached showing plate #23.

Appendix VIII – Fractional Currency Plate Numbers

Below at left is an FR1230 with plate #15.2nd and 3rd issue. 2nd and 3rd issue fractional notes had the plate numbers engraved within subject field. Plate numbers on the aforementioned issues were engraved in the intersecting quadrant of 4 notes as nicely demonstrated below right by this 3rd issue FR1238 with plate #26:

Shown below is a 2nd issue FR1232 with face plate #243

Below is a 2nd issue FR1249 with plate #29 on the reverse:

In 1972 Martin Gengerke first published fractional sheet plate numbers in *SPMC Paper Money* (Vol. 11, Whole #42, Page 80). Previous to Martin's article being published, it was believed that fires destroyed all the original records. Fortunately while Martin was researching BEP archives, he discovered an old journal of the 2nd and 3rd issues only. While not complete, it was an important discovery regarding plate number accounting. Please note adjoining charts of 2nd and 3rd issue sheet plate numbers.

Seal Plate Numbers

4th issue fractional notes were the first time treasury seals were employed. Consequently note production increased to 3 plates for the finished product. They are as follows:

Appendix VIII – Fractional Currency Plate Numbers

1. Reverse subject sheet plates had the plate number engraved in the selvage.

2. Obverse subject sheet plates also had the plate number engraved on the selvage.

3. Obverse seal plates contained just the BEP seals and in most series included a seal plate number. These seal plate numbers were engraved and they often showed up within the subject field.

However, seal plate numbers are not on all 4th issue notes – they appear in the subject field on the 10¢ (FR1257-61), 15¢ (FR1267-71), 25¢ (FR1301-1307) and 50¢ Lincoln (FR1374). 4th issue 50¢ Stanton (FR1376) has either no seal plate number or it was engraved in the outer margins. The 50¢ Dexter (FR1379) did not have a seal plate number but included position numbers on the obverse subject plate that showed up on the finished note.Plate numbers that show up on the obverse of 4th issue fractionals are almost always seal plate numbers. Shown below is an FR1303 will seal plate #11

Shown below is a Stanton (FR1376) with inverted sheet plate #21 on the bottom right. They are extremely rare and only exist because the selvage of the note was untrimmed.

Appendix VIII – Fractional Currency Plate Numbers

Shown below is one of the few known sheet plate number on any 4th issue reverse. It is an FR1301 (4th issue – 25¢) with mirrored plate #6:

No previous records of 4th issue seal plates existed, but with research on the existing 4th issue notes currently in the marketplace a nearly complete listing of 4th issue seal plate numbers was pieced together. Please note the adjoining chart of all the known 4th issue seal plate numbers.

5th issue fractionals have the sheet plate numbers on the reverse in the selvage. While both 4th and 5th issue fractionals have treasury seals, seal plate numbers only show up for the 4th issue. 5th issue fractionals, like the 4th issue Dexter, employed position numbers on the obverse plate. Any plate numbers on 5th issue reverses notes are exceedingly rare. Shown below is an FR1381 with subject plate #39 on the selvedge.

ppendix VIII – Fractional Currency Plate Numbers

SECOND ISSUE FRACTIONAL PLATE NUMBERS

late	Type	Plate	Type	Plate	Type	Plate	Type	Plate	Type	Plate	Type	Plate	Type
1	25¢ rx	41	50¢ ob	81	5¢ rx	121	50¢ ob	161	10¢ rx	201	25¢ ob	241	25¢ ob
2	5¢ ob	42	5¢ ob	82	10¢ rx	122	50¢ ob	162	5¢ ob	202	25¢ ob	242	25¢ rx
3	5¢ ob	43	50¢ ob	83	25¢ ob	123	50¢ ob P	163	50¢ rx	203	25¢ ob	243	5¢ ob
4	5¢ rx P	44	10¢ ob	84	10¢ ob P	124	50¢ rx	164	10¢ ob	204	25¢ ob	244	25¢ rx
5	5¢ ob	45	50¢ ob	85	10¢ ob	125	25¢ ob	165	5¢ rx	205	10¢ ob	245	25¢ ob
6	5¢ rx	46	50¢ ob	86	5¢ rx	126	25¢ ob	166	10¢ ob	206	25¢ ob	246	5¢ rx
7	5¢ ob	47	25¢ ob	87	50¢ rx	127	50¢ rx	167	10¢ rx	207	25¢ rx	247	25¢ ob
8	25¢ rx	48	25¢ ob	88	10¢ rx P	128	25¢ rx	168	10¢ rx	208	25¢ rx	248	25¢ ob
9	25¢ ob	49	25¢ ob	89	25¢ rx	129	25¢ ob	169	10¢ ob	209	25¢ ob	249	25¢ rx
10	5¢ rx	50	25¢ ob	90	50¢ ob	130	50¢ rx	170	5¢ rx	210	25¢ ob	250	25¢ rx
11	25¢ ob	51	5¢ ob	91	5¢ ob	131	25¢ rx	171	10¢ ob	211	25¢ ob	251	25¢ ob
12	5¢ rx	52	10¢ ob	92	5¢ rx	132	50¢ rx	172	5¢ ob	212	25¢ ob	252	25¢ ob
13	10¢ rx	53	25¢ ob	93	10¢ rx	133	50¢ rx	173	10¢ rx	213	25¢ ob	253	25¢ rx
14	10¢ ob	54	25¢ ob	94	25¢ ob	134	50¢ rx	174	5¢ ob	214	25¢ ob	254	25¢ ob
15	25¢ rx	55	50¢ ob	95	50¢ ob	135	25¢ rx	175	5¢ ob	215	25¢ ob	255	25¢ ob
16	50¢ rx	56	10¢ ob	96	10¢ ob	136	25¢ rx	176	10¢ ob	216	25¢ rx	256	25¢ rx
17	50¢ ob	57	10¢ ob	97	10¢ ob	137	25¢ ob	177	5¢ rx	217	25¢ ob	257	25¢ rx
18	50¢ rx	58	5¢ ob	98	5¢ ob	138	25¢ rx	178	5¢ rx	218	25¢ ob	258	25¢ ob
19	50¢ rx	59	50¢ rx	99	25¢ ob	139	50¢ rx	179	10¢ ob	219	25¢ rx	259	25¢ rx
20	10¢ rx	60	5¢ ob	100	10¢ rx	140	50¢ rx	180	25¢ ob	220	25¢ ob	260	25¢ rx
21	50¢ rx	61	25¢ rx	101	5¢ rx	141	25¢ rx	181	10¢ ob	221	25¢ ob	261	25¢ ob
22	25¢ rx	62	50¢ rx	102	10¢ rx	142	10¢ ob	182	10¢ ob	222	25¢ rx	262	25¢ rx
23	50¢ ob	63	5¢ ob	103	10¢ rx	143	10¢ ob	183	10¢ ob	223	25¢ ob	263	25¢ rx
24	25¢ ob	64	50¢ rx	104	5¢ rx	144	10¢ rx	184	10¢ ob	224	25¢ ob	264	25¢ rx
25	25¢ rx	65	10¢ ob	105	5¢ rx	145	10¢ ob	185	10¢ ob	225	25¢ rx	265	25¢ ob
26	50¢ ob	66	10¢ ob	106	10¢ rx	146	10¢ ob	186	5¢ ob	226	25¢ rx	266	25¢ rx
27	50¢ rx	67	50¢ ob	107	5¢ rx	147	10¢ rx	187	5¢ ob	227	25¢ ob	267	25¢ rx
28	25¢ rx	68	10¢ rx	108	5¢ ob	148	10¢ rx	188	10¢ ob	228	25¢ ob	268	25¢ rx
29	10¢ rx	69	5¢ ob	109	5¢ ob	149	10¢ rx	189	10¢ rx	229	5¢ rx	269	25¢ ob
30	25¢ ob	70	25¢ rx	110	5¢ rx	150	5¢ ob	190	5¢ rx	230	25¢ rx	270	25¢ ob
31	50¢ ob	71	10¢ ob	111	5¢ rx	151	50¢ rx	191	5¢ ob	231	25¢ rx	271	25¢ rx
32	50¢ rx	72	5¢ ob	112	5¢ rx	152	25¢ ob	192	10¢ ob	232	5¢ ob	272	10¢ ob
33	10¢ ob	73	25¢ ob	113	50¢ ob P	153	5¢ rx	193	5¢ rx	233	25¢ ob	273	5¢ ob
34	25¢ rx	74	50¢ rx	114	25¢ rx	154	5¢ rx	194	5¢ ob	234	25¢ ob	274	10¢ rx
35	25¢ ob	75	50¢ ob	115	5¢ rx	155	10¢ rx	195	5¢ rx	235	25¢ ob	275	10¢ ob
36	50¢ ob	76	25¢ rx	116	25¢ rx P	156	5¢ ob	196	5¢ ob	236	5¢ ob	276	25¢ ob
37	25¢ ob	77	25¢ rx	117	25¢ rx	157	5¢ ob	197	10¢ ob	237	25¢ ob	277	25¢ ob
38	50¢ rx	78	5¢ rx	118	5¢ ob	158	5¢ rx	198	10¢ ob	238	25¢ ob	278	5¢ rx
39	50¢ ob	79	5¢ ob	119	50¢ rx	159	5¢ rx	199	10¢ ob	239	25¢ ob	279	25¢ ob
40	50¢ ob	80	10¢ rx	120	25¢ ob	160	10¢ ob	200	10¢ ob	240	5¢ ob	280	10¢ ob

- Note cut from plate proof S - Plate for wide margin proof

Appendix VIII – Fractional Currency Plate Numbers

SECOND ISSUE FRACTIONAL PLATE NUMBERS (cont.)

Plate	Type	Plate	Type	Plate	Type	Plate	Type	Plate	Type	Plate	Type	Plate	Type
281	5¢ rx	291	10¢ ob	301	5¢ ob	311	10¢ ob	321	10¢ ob	331	10¢ ob	341	50¢ ob S
282	10¢ ob	292	10¢ rx	302	10¢ rx	312	10¢ ob	322	10¢ rx	332	10¢ ob	342	50¢ rx S
283	5¢ rx	293	5¢ rx	303	5¢ ob	313	10¢ rx	323	10¢ ob	333	10¢ rx	343	5¢ ob
284	10¢ rx	294	25¢ ob	304	5¢ rx	314	5¢ rx	324	10¢ ob	334	5¢ ob S	344	5¢ ob
285	5¢ ob	295	5¢ ob	305	10¢ ob	315	10¢ ob	325	10¢ ob	335	5¢ rx S	345	25¢ rx S
286	25¢ rx P	296	5¢ ob	306	10¢ rx	316	10¢ ob	326	10¢ rx	336	10¢ ob S		
287	5¢ ob	297	10¢ ob	307	5¢ rx	317	10¢ ob	327	10¢ rx	337	10¢ rx S		
288	25¢ ob	298	10¢ ob	308	10¢ rx	318	5¢ rx	328	10¢ rx	338	5¢ ob		
289	10¢ ob	299	10¢ ob	309	10¢ ob	319	10¢ rx	329	10¢ rx	339	25¢ ob S		
290	10¢ ob	300	5¢ rx	310	10¢ ob	320	10¢ ob	330	10¢ ob	340	5¢ ob		

P- Note cut from plate proof S - Plate for wide margin proof

THIRD ISSUE FRACTIONAL PLATE NUMBERS

Third Issue Three Cent Plates

Plate	Types
1-28	Reverses
29 - 61	Obverses, light curtain
62 - 68	Obverses, dark curtain
69	Wide margin obverse, dark curtain
70	Wide margin reverse
71	Wide margin obverse, light curtain

Variety without pearls - plates 32 and 35

Plate 69 had one sample note cut out

Third Issue Five Cent Plates

Plate	Description	Plate	Description	Plate	Description
1	rev	21	obv	41	obv
2	rev	22	obv	42	obv
3	rev P	23	obv	43	obv
4	rev	24	obv	44	rev
5	rev	25	obv	45	obv
6	rev	26	obv	46	obv
7	rev	27	obv	47	rev
8	rev	28	rev	48	rev
9	rev	29	obv	49	rev
10	rev	30	obv	50	obv
11	rev	31	rev	51	rev
12	rev	32	obv P	52	obv
13	rev	33	rev	53	rev
14	obv P	34	rev	54	obv
15	obv	35	obv	55	obv
16	obv	36	rev	56	rev
17	obv	37	obv	57	rev
18	obv	38	rev	58	rev
19	obv	39	obv	59	rev
20	obv	40	rev	60	rev
61	Obverse, wide margin				
62	Reverse, wide margin, one note cut out				

P - Note cut from plate proof

Appendix VIII – Fractional Currency Plate Numbers

THIRD ISSUE FRACTIONAL

TEN CENT PLATE NUMBERS

Plate	Description	Plate	Description	Plate	Description
1	rev	46	rev	91	obv
2	rev	47	rev	92	obv
3	rev	48	obv	93	obv
4	rev	49	obv	94	obv
5	rev	50	obv	95	obv
6	rev	51	rev	96	obv
7	obv	52	obv	97	rev
8	obv N	53	obv	98	rev
9	obv N	54	obv	99	rev
10	obv N	55	rev	100	rev
11	obv N	56	obv	101	rev
12	obv N	57	rev	102	rev
13	obv N	58	obv	103	obv
14	obv N	59	obv	104	obv
15	obv	60	rev	105	obv
16	rev	61	obv	106	obv
17	rev P	62	obv	107	rev
18	rev	63	obv	108	obv
19	rev	64	rev S	109	rev
20	rev	65	rev	110	obv
21	rev	66	obv S	111	obv
22	rev	67	obv	112	obv
23	obv P	68	obv	113	obv
24	obv	69	obv	114	obv
25	rev	70	rev	115	obv
26	obv	71	obv N S	116	obv
27	rev	72	rev	117	obv
28	obv	73	rev	118	obv
29	rev	74	obv	119	obv
30	rev	75	obv	120	obv
31	obv	76	obv	121	obv
32	rev	77	obv	122	obv
33	obv	78	obv	123	obv
34	rev	79	obv	124	obv
35	obv	80	rev	125	obv
36	obv	81	rev	126	obv
37	obv	82	rev	127	obv
38	obv	83	rev	128	obv P
39	obv	84	rev	129	obv
40	rev	85	rev	130	rev P
41	obv	86	obv	131	rev
42	rev	87	obv	132	rev
43	obv	88	obv		
44	obv	89	obv		
45	obv	90	obv		

S - Plate for wide margin specimens
N- Plates without engraved signatures
P - Note cut from plate proof

Appendix VIII – Fractional Currency Plate Numbers

THIRD ISSUE FRACTIONAL

TWENTY FIVE CENT PLATE NUMBERS

Plate	Description	Plate	Description	Plate	Description	Plate	Description
1	rev P	38	obv	75	obv	112	obv
2	rev	39	obv	76	obv	113	obv
3	rev	40	obv	77	obv	114	obv
4	rev	41	obv	78	obv	115	obv
5	rev	42	obv	79	obv	116	obv P
6	rev	43	obv	80	rev	117	obv
7	rev	44	obv	81	obv	118	obv
8	rev	45	obv	82	rev	119	obv
9	rev	46	rev	83	rev	120	obv
10	rev	47	obv	84	rev S	121	rev
11	rev	48	rev	85	obv S	122	rev
12	rev	49	obv	86	obv	123	rev
13	rev	50	rev	87	obv	124	rev
14	rev	51	obv	88	obv	125	rev
15	rev	52	obv	89	obv	126	rev
16	rev	53	rev	90	rev	127	obv
17	rev	54	rev	91	obv	128	obv
18	rev	55	obv	92	rev	129	obv
19	rev	56	rev	93	obv	130	obv
20	rev	57	rev	94	obv	131	obv
21	rev	58	rev	95	obv	132	obv
22	rev	59	obv	96	obv	133	obv
23	rev	60	rev	97	obv	134	obv
24	rev	61	obv	98	obv	135	obv
25	rev	62	obv	99	obv	136	obv
26	obv	63	rev	100	obv	137	obv
27	obv	64	obv	101	rev	138	obv
28	obv	65	rev	102	rev	139	obv
29	obv	66	obv	103	rev	140	obv
30	obv	67	obv	104	rev	141	obv
31	obv	68	rev	105	rev	142	obv
32	obv	69	obv	106	rev	143	obv
33	obv	70	obv	107	obv	144	obv
34	obv	71	obv	108	obv	145	obv
35	obv	72	obv P	109	obv	146	obv
36	obv	73	obv	110	obv		
37	obv	74	obv	111	obv		

Plate 144 had the letter 'a' 7mm to the lower right

S - Plate for wide margin specimens

P - Note cut from plate proof

Appendix VIII – Fractional Currency Plate Numbers

THIRD ISSUE FRACTIONAL PLATE NUMBERS

50¢ Justice Obverses, and Type 1 Reverses

Plate	Description	Plate	Description	Plate	Description	Plate	Description
1	rev	26	obv	51	obv	76	obv S
2	obv N	27	rev	52	rev	77	obv
3	obv N	28	rev	53	obv	78	obv
4	rev	29	rev	54	obv	79	obv
5	obv	30	rev	55	obv	80	obv
6	rev	31	obv	56	rev	81	obv
7	obv	32	rev	57	obv	82	obv
8	obv	33	rev	58	rev	83	obv
9	rev	34	obv	59	obv	84	obv
10	rev	35	rev	60	obv	85	obv
11	rev	36	rev	61	rev	86	obv
12	rev	37	rev	62	obv	87	obv S
13	obv	38	obv	63	obv	88	rev S
14	obv	39	obv	64	obv	89	rev
15	rev	40	rev	65	obv	90	rev
16	rev	41	rev	66	rev	91	rev
17	obv	42	obv	67	obv	92	rev
18	rev	43	obv	68	rev	93	obv N S
19	obv P	44	rev	69	obv	94	rev
20	rev	45	obv	70	rev P		
21	rev	46	rev	71	rev		
22	rev	47	obv	72	rev		
23	obv	48	obv	73	obv		
24	rev	49	obv	74	obv		
25	rev	50	rev	75	obv		

N - No engraved signatures
S - Plate for wide margin specimen
P - Note cut from plate proof

50¢ Spinner Obverse Plates

Plates numbered from 1 to 56, #'s 1 and 42 had no signatures, and plates 41 and 42 were for wide margin proofs.
Note cut from proof of plate #1

50¢ Type 2 Reverse Plates

Plates numbered from 1 to 31; plate 21 was for wide margin proofs.
Proof of plate 10 had 1 note cut out.

Appendix VIII – Fractional Currency Plate Numbers

FRACTIONAL PLATE NUMBERS

Auxiliary Numbering System for Wide Margin Proofs

	Plates 1 to 8 are second issue, others third issue		15¢ Grant & Sherman Plates
Plate #	**Type**	**Plate #**	**Description**
1	5¢ obverse	1	Wide margin reverses, 8 subjects
2	10¢ obverse	2 P	Wide margin obverses, no signatures, 8 subjects
3	10¢ reverse	3	Wide margin obverses, engraved signatures, 8 subjects
4	25¢ obverse	4 P	reverse, 12 subjects
5	50¢ obverse	5	reverse, 12 subjects
6	50¢ reverse	6	obverse, 12 subjects
7	5¢ reverse	7	obverse, 12 subjects
8	25¢ reverse	8	reverse, 12 subjects
9	10¢ obverse, engraved signatures	9	reverse, 12 subjects
10	3¢ obverse, dark curtain	10	obverse, 12 subjects
11	10¢ reverse	11	obverse, 12 subjects
12	25¢ reverse	12	reverse, 12 subjects
13	25¢ obverse	13	reverse, 12 subjects
14	3¢ reverse	14	reverse, 12 subjects
15	50¢ reverse , type 1	15 P	reverse, 12 subjects
16	50¢ Justice obverse, engraved signatures	16	obverse, 12 subjects
17	50¢ Spinner obverse, engraved signatures	17	obverse, 12 subjects
18	5¢ obverse	18	obverse, 12 subjects
19	5¢ reverse	19 P	obverse, 12 subjects
20			
21	50¢ reverse, type 2		

P - Note cut from plate proof

ppendix VIII – Fractional Currency Plate Numbers

Inverted and Mirrored Plate Numbers

iedberg #	Inverted Plate #	Position	Reference
1226	2	Reverse	R Melamed Collection (2)
1230	28 (900 rotated)	Obverse	Private Collection
1255	inverted 83	Reverse	R Melamed Collection
1255	inverted & mirror 83	Reverse	Valentine Reference, Rmelamed Collection
1256	inverted & mirror 83	Reverse	Valentine Reference
1259	4	Obverse	Rmelamed Collection, RM Smythe 10/04 Lot 2702
1259	18	Obverse	eBay Item number: 3928205557
1259	20	Obverse	2x R. Melamed Collection, lot 2760 Goldberg 2/2001
1259	21	Obverse	lot 688 - CAA 1/97-R. Melamed collection
1259	32	Obverse	R Melamed Collection (2)
1259	33	Obverse	Valentine Reference
1259	34	Obverse	lot 898 CAA 2/02-R. Melamed Collection
1267	mirror 5	Obverse	#5310 CAA 9/01 & Valentine reference &R Melamed x2
267 Sheet	mirror 5	Obverse	Lot 1005 Stack's 5/04
1267	20	Obverse	ebay : 3922038088
1269	4	Obverse	Private Collection
1269	10	Obverse	R Melamed Collection
1271	7	Obverse	R Melamed Collection
1294	partial 48	Reverse	Private Collection
1294	6x	Obverse	R Melamed Collection
1301	mirror 6	Reverse	R Melamed Collection from O'Mara 5/05 CAA Auction Lot 15785
1303	10	Obverse	#702, NASCA 5/77
1303	partial 54	unknown	Private collection; lot 841 CAA 9/02
1307	Inverted 2	Obverse	R Melamed Collection
1316	partial 3	unknown	Private collection
1320	12	Obverse	Lot 91, Glazer Mail Bid Sale #1
1328	Mirror 1	Obverse	Ref By Richard Jacobson
1331	partial 6	Reverse	#5270 CAA 9/01-RM Collection
1331	mirror 21	reverse	R Melamed Collection
1332	32	Reverse	R Melamed Collection; lot 2031 Lyn Knight 6/04; lot 502 Stack 10/07
1334	32	Reverse	R Melamed Collection
1336	32 partial	Reverse	#819 CAA 2/02*, #145 1/95, #15214 9/04*, Lot 16042 May 2005 O'mara Sale
1335	44	Reverse	Private collection
1336	partial 44	Reverse	#16691 CAA 1/03
1337	partial 44	Reverse	Private collection
1337	29	Reverse	HA lot 14111 4/10
1343	Partial 36	Reverse	Rmelamed Collection from Lot 16052 May 2005 O'Mara Sale
1338	partial 44	Reverse	R Melamed Collection
1358	mirror 21	Reverse	R Melamed Collection(2) , lot 15518 CAA 9/05 sale; Lot 32089 HA 5/17/11
1360	29	Reverse	R Melamed Collection
1362	mirror 21	Reverse	lot 873 CAA 2002 - RM Collection
1362	12	Reverse	Private Collection
1362	44	Reverse	ebay 250782553792 3/11
362 w/inv urcharge	18	Reverse	Valentine Reference
1363	12	Reverse	Private collection; lot 841 CAA 9/02, Lot 933 Stacks 5/04, Lot 77 Stacks 6/05

Appendix VIII – Fractional Currency Plate Numbers

Inverted and Mirrored Plate Numbers (cont.)

Friedberg #	Inverted Plate #	Position	Reference
1363	32	Reverse	R Melamed Collection
1363	partial 20	Reverse	lot 16744 - CAA 1/03
1363	22	Reverse	R Melamed Collection
1363	partial 2	Reverse	could be plate # 20, 21, 22 or 29 - RM Collection
1363	32	Reverse	R Melamed Collection
1364	22	Reverse	Lot 15478 1/05 FUN
1364	22	Reverse	R Melamed Collection
1364	29	Reverse	Valentine Reference
1365	20	Reverse	RM Collection (2); Lot 935 Stack's 5/04
1365	12 partial	Reverse	Valentine Reference
1365	29 partial	Reverse	R Melamed Collection
1365	22 partial	Reverse	Lot 21260 6/15 CAA internet auction and now w/ RM
1365	41	Reverse	Lot 79 Stack 6/05, R Melamed Collection
1365	52	Reverse	Lot 472 10/07; R Melamed Collection
1368	12	Reverse	R Melamed Collection
1368	32	Reverse	lot 884 CAA 2/2002; lot 938 Stacks 5/04
1368	44 partial	Reverse	Lot 15535 CAA 9/05 sale
1369	12 partial	Reverse	Heritage Lot 15388 FUN 2011
1369	29	Reverse	Private Collection
1369	32	Reverse	R Melamed Collection
1371	mirror 21	Reverse	Private Collection
1371	29	Reverse	Several Exist
1371	42	Obverse	Valentine Reference
1372	partial 22	Obverse	R Melamed Collection
1372	29	Reverse	Lot 13110 CAA 9/07, Lot 626 EAHA 3/10 - RM Collection
1372	29	Reverse	Lot 3512 Fun 1/2011
1376	21	Obverse	Jan 2010 Heritage - Lot 13560
1232SP-WM-OBV	4x Partial		Private collection (2nd digit is not definable)
1232SP-WM-OBV	mirror 334 partial		R Melamed Collection
1232SP-WM-REV	mirror 335		R Melamed Collection
1251SP-WM-REV	11		Several Exist
1255SP-WM-REV	11		Several Exist
1283SP-WM-OBV	mirror 339		Private Collection
1294SP-WM-OBV	13 (900 rotated)		2 known
CFT1295	mirror 51	reverse	Counterfeit - private Collection

Appendix X – Auction Catalogs and Retail Lists

There is a wealth of information to be found in auction catalogs and dealer retail lists. There will be notes or fractionalrelated items that haven't been seen publicly since appearing in an auction, perhaps 100 years ago. The catalogs of the last 50 or so years may feature pictures, helping a researcher trace the history or pedigree of a specific note through careful matching of the note's attributes (edges, surcharges and alignment, fiber strands, etc).

What follows is a sampling of some materials a fractional enthusiast will find interesting. Since the early 1980s there has been an explosion of useful catalogs, too numerous to list here. If you have a favorite list or catalog you would like to be considered, please contact me so I may include it in my notes for future editions.

American Auction Association: Auction Catalog:
—Matt Rothert Sale, November 16-17, 1973.

Bowers and Merena: Auction Catalogs:
—Herman Halpern Sale, March 24, 1995.

Bowers and Ruddy: Auction Catalogs:
—Matt Rothert Collection, November 16, 1973.
—James A. Doolittle & Robert A. Russell Sale, June 20-22, 1977.

Chapman, S.H. and C.: Auction Catalogs:
—C.S. Wilcox Sale, November 6-7, 1901.
—Monroe Friedman Sale, June 3, 1903.
—C.S. Wilcox Sale, February 15, 1904.

Currency Auction of America: Auction Catalogs:
—Wayne Liechty Sale, January 7, 1994
—Martin Gengerke Sale, January 6, 1995
—Milton R. Friedberg Sale, January 10, 1997
—Michael Marchioni Sale, January 7, 2000
—(Numerous other catalogs from this auction company)

Denly, Tom: List, Bank Note Reporter; July, 2001.

French's Auctions: Auction Catalogs:
—May, 1954
—February, 1957
—May, 1957
—May, 1966

Frossard, Ed.: Special List No. 8 - Unique Collection of Essays & Proofs of United States Fractional Currency, Oct. 1, 1893

Len & Jean Glazer: Fractional Currency, Inc.: Auction Sale No. 2; June 17-18, 1980.

Glazer, Len: List #8, 1976;

Appendix X – Auction Catalogs and Retail Lists

Kosoff, A., Auction Catalog:
—M. Burgett Sale, ANA Convention, 1958.

Kravitz, Robert J.: Lists:
—#1, Rob's Coins and Currency, 1976;
—Rob's Coins and Currency, June, 2000;
—Rob's Coins and Currency, June, 2001.

Max B. Mehl: Auction Catalog:
—Albert Grinnell Collection, June 15, 1943.

Merkin, Lester: List #4, 1963; Auction Catalogs:
—Wayte Raymond Sale, October 6, 1972;
—Isadore Herman Sale, September 12, 1974.

NASCA: Auction Catalog:
—Philip Chase Sale, May 5, 1977.
—T. James Clark Sale, June 6, 1978.
—Dr. Joseph Vacca Sale, April. 27, 1981.
—Rocky Rockholt Sale, Sept. 12, 1981.

New Netherlands: Auction Catalog:
—Philip Straus Collection, June 16, 1959.

Stack's: Auction Catalogs:
—Dr. Frank A. Limpert Sale, September 24, 1955
—Alan May Sale, May 6, 1992
—Herman Halpern Sale, March 17, 1993
—John J. Ford Collection", Part III, May, 2004
—John J. Ford Collection", Part XI, June, 2005
—John J. Ford Collection", Part XIX, October, 2007
—(Numerous other catalogs from this auction company)

Superior Galleries: Auction Catalogs:
—John Fraser Collection, January 2, 1982

IMPORTANT DATES IN POSTAGE & FRACTIONAL CURRENCY HISTORY AND WHAT HAPPENED IN THE CIVIL WAR ON THAT DATE

Saturday - August 10th, 1861

Union General Nathaniel Lyon knows that he does not have enough men (just 8,000) to protect the City of Springfield Missouri from the Confederate forces. He therefore sets out to attack at Wilson's Creek hoping to at least delay the advancing Confederate force of 15,000 men, until General Fremont can send help from St. Louis. Lyon divides his troops into two columns, one under Sigel to attack from the rear, and the other led by General Lyon to attack from the front. General Lyon is killed on Bloody Ridge while at the head of the 1st Iowa Regiment. Union losses are 223 killed and 721 wounded, the Confederate losses are 421 killed and 1,300 wounded. Even though Wilson Creek is a significant Confederate victory, General McCulloch's army received a severe mauling and therefore was unable to pursue the retreating Union Army.

The Hoarding of Coins Begins

After the Union losses at Bull Run and Wilson's Creek the Union now realizes that it could be a long war. Many people start saving copper, silver and gold coins because of their intrinsic value.

Saturday, December 28th, 1861

The New York banks stopped specie payments. "Specie Payment" means the banks would not redeem paper money for coins. Because of the Civil War people were already hoarding gold, silver and copper coins.

That Same Day Out West:

At Mount Zion Missouri, the 3rd Missouri Union Cavalry scattered a rebel force of 900. The Union forces lost 5 killed and 63 wounded. The rebels lost 25 killed and had 175 wounded.

Sunday, April 27th, 1862 – Naval Battle

The Confederate blockade runner Bermuda is captured by the Union ship U.S.S. Mergdita. The cargo was on it's way to the Confederacy, many rifles, barrels of powder and cases of swords. Also included in the cargo was 752 reams of CSA watermarked paper. Since the paper was a prize of War, the Treasury Department bought the CSA paper at 56¢ per ream. The CSA watermark paper was used to print 2nd and 3rd issue fractional currency proofs (specimens). Therefore, all of the CSA watermarked notes were at one time in a Naval battle in the Civil War!

Appendix XI – Important Dates

Thursday, July 17th, 1862

President Lincoln signed a law allowing the use of postage stamps as money. This and Spinner's idea of postage stamps on Treasury paper was the birth of Postage Currency!

That Same Day in the Civil War:

Colonel Morgan's Confederate raiders make a surprise attack on Northern troops and capture Cynthiania, Kentucky. There were 17 Union solders and 24 Confederates killed.

Thursday, August 21st, 1862

The printing of Postage Currency starts today, with the printing of the straight edge, no monogram notes. The Treasury distributes a small amount of these to Army Paymasters.

That Same Day in the Civil War:

Union troops capture almost 2,000 and kill over 700 Confederate troops at the Rappahannock River.

The Week of September 15th, 1862

The printing of the 1st Issue of perforated, no monogram notes started.

That Same Time in the Civil War:

Wednesday, September 17th, 1862 – Battle of Antietem

The Union General Burnside attacks the Confederates Southern right flank, pushing the Confederate troops to the side and crossing "Burnside" Bridge and advancing on Antietem. They are finally stopped by Confederate General Hill. Both sides had very heavy casualties: the North had 2,108 killed, 9,549 wounded and 753 men were missing; the South had 2,700 killed, 9,024 wounded and 2,000 or so men missing! Antietem is considered the bloodiest single day of the war. So no side really won, but the Union forces did stop General Lee's invasion of the North

Act of March 3rd, 1863

This Act authorized the printing of the Second Issue and officially changed the name from Postage Currency to Fractional Currency. The change came about because of two things: may notes of the First Issue were counterfeited; second, the cost would be less if the Government printed the notes themselves.

Civil War News That Same Day:

To help the War effort, Congress passes the Conscription Act, which calls for the enlistment in military service all male citizens between 20 and 45 years of age. The service will be for 3 years.

Appendix XI – Important Dates

May 27th, 1863 - End of Postage Currency

The Postage Currency became the "pocket change" of the Northern states, even on the Pacific coast. There was no small change shortages as the Postage Currency filled these needs. The Act of March 3rd, 1863 provided for the new Fractional Currency but was restricted to only $ 50,000,000 combined issues outstanding of Postage Currency and the newly proposed Fractional Currency. This started the withdrawal of the Postage Currency. By the end of 1863 the Treasury reported 31,000,000 pieces of Postage currency destroyed.

Civil War News That Same Day:

Union General Banks begins the siege of Port Hudson, Louisiana, since the initial attack was fought off by the Confederates under General Gardner.

Saturday, October 10th, 1863

The Second Issue printing of Fractional Currency starts. First to be printed are the fiber paper notes. The fiber notes were stopped; they were hard to print (hold the ink), and they split apart too easy.

Civil War News That Same Day:

Some minor skirmishes take place along the Rapidan in Virginia as General Lee tries to maneuver behind the Union Army under General Meade.

Thursday, November 10th, 1864

The printing of the Second Issue fractionals began on regular bank note type paper.

Civil War News That Same Day:

After his defeat at Cedar Creek, Jubal Early leads what's left of his Confederate forces to harass General Sheridan's Union Army in the Shenendoah Valley.

Monday, December 5th, 1864

The first notes of the 3rd Issue are printed on this date; the first fiber paper Justice notes. Fr. 1351, Fr. 1352, Fr. 1353, Fr. 1354 and Fr. 1357 all have red backs and surcharges of "S-2-6-4".

Civil War News That Same Day:

General Thomas prepares to attack the Confederate Army at Nashville under General Hood. There is bad weather (freezing rain), so General Thomas waits...

Monday, January 23rd, 1865

The release of the 3¢ Third Issue fractional currency begins. This note is not only the smallest denomination, but the smallest

Appendix XI – Important Dates

note in size at 39mm by 64mm.

Civil War News That Same Day:

Eleven Confederate ships sail down the James River, hoping to attack the Union Fleet concentrated at Fort Fisher. Because of the obstructions laid on Grant's orders six months earlier, four of the ships run aground. At dawn they come under fire from the Union guns in Fort Parsons. One ship is destroyed and the rest turn tail and escape, abandoning their attack.

Tuesday, February 21st, 1865

The first of just 16,000 red back 25¢ Third Issue notes (Fr. 1291 and Fr. 1292) are released.

Civil War News That Same Day:

Confederate General Bragg orders the evacuation of his troops from Wilmington, North Carolina, which is the last major Confederate port. Union General Cox and his men are closing in fast from the West.

Friday, March 3rd, 1865

Congress passed the Act providing for a three-cent coin of 75% copper - 25% nickel to replace the three cent fractional currency.

Civil War News on Thursday, March 2nd, 1865:

George Armstrong Custer's 5,000 strong calvary division attacks Jubal Early's entrenched 2,000 strong Confederate position at Waynes Borough in the Shenandoah Valley. Most of the Confederates are taken prisoner - over 1,000 men along with 200 wagons of supplies. This was a major Union victory.

Wednesday, March 22nd, 1865

The 25¢ Third Issue green back (M-2-6-5 surcharged) fiber paper notes start to be issued. They are the Fr. 1297, Fr. 1298, Fr. 1299 and the Fr. 1300.

Civil War News That Same Day:

Union General Wilson with 13,000 men crosses the Tennessee River from Waterloo, Alabama toward Selma, Alabama to destroy one of the South's last munition factories.

Wednesday, April 5th, 1865

The last of the 3¢ Third Issue notes are released since the denomination was abolished by the Act of March 3rd, 1865.

Civil War News That Same Day:

General Lee moves his army towards Farmville, VA. Out of supplies, he hopes to feed his hungry army there. His further retreat is blocked at the Danville railroad. The War will end soon.

Bibliography

Bishop, Chris and Drury, Ian: *1400 Days: The Civil War Day by Day*, 1990.

Blake, George H.: *United States Paper Money*, 1908.

Breen, Walter: "History of the Fractional Currency Specimen Sets", *The Numismatic Scrapbook Magazine*, January and February Issues, 1964.

Fractional Currency articles, *Numismatic News Weekly*, July 18, July 25, August 15, September 19, September 26, 1972.

Carothers, Neil: *Fractional Money*, 1930

Christoph, Art and Krause, Chet: "United States Postage and Fractional Currencys". A reprint from *The Numismatic News*, 1958.

Civil War Almanac, The: United States Congressional Record: Miscellanies Document #163, April, 1876.

Heritage Currency Auctions of America: The *Tom O'Mara Collection*, May, 2005

Friedberg, Milton R: *The Encyclopedia of United States Fractional and Postage Currency*, 1978.

Friedberg, Robert, Arthur and Ira: *Paper Money of the United States*, 19th edition, 2010.

Gengerke, Martin: "Fractional Currency Plate Information," *Paper Money*, Vol 11, No. 02, Whole 42, March-April, 1972.

Gragg, Rod: *Civil War Quiz and Fact Book*, 1985.

Heath, Laban: *Heath's Infallible Counterfeit Detector*, 1870.

Limpert, Dr. F.A.: *United States Postage and Fractional Currency*, 1946.

—*Classified List of Postage and Fractional Currency*, 1947.

Pine Tree Rare Coin Auction: September 18, 1974.

Raymond, Wayte: *The Standard Paper Money Catalog - Part II: United States Notes and Fractional Currency*, 1954.

Reinfeld, Fred: *The Story of Civil War Money*, 1959.

Rothert, Matt: *A Guidebook of United States Fractional Currency*, 1963.

Schultz, Walter F.: *Schultz's Checking List of Fractional Currency*, 1935.

Scientific American: March 26, 1870.

Stack's: *"John J. Ford Collection"*, *Part III*, May, 2004; *Part XI*, June, 2005; *Part XIX*, October, 2007.

Tebben, Gerald: "Paper Money Use Flourished During Civil War Hardships", *Coin World*, March 29, 1993.

United States Department of the Treasury: *History of the Bureau of Engraving and Printing*, 1962.

Valentine, D. W.: *Fractional Currency of the United States, Volumes One and Two*, 1924.

Glossary

AU Almost Uncirculated. Notes that only have one fold or a couple of corner-tip folds

Bleaching Processing of a note with a diluted amount of bleach. Used to artificially brighten notes. Unfortunately, this damages the notes and they will always look and smell bleached.

Burn Holes See "Ink Burns"

Centering Refers to the margins on a note both front and back. A note with perfect margins would look as if the design of the note was in a picture frame.

CSA Paper Paper that was to be used for Confederate States of America bank notes, captured by Union ships and used for printing some Proof Fractional Currency Notes.

CHCU Choice, Crisp, Uncirculated. A new note, but not quite GEM. Centering may be just a little off, e.g. three good margins and one close margin.

CU Crisp Uncirculated. No signs of circulation, no folds. May have counting signs or wrinkles.

Cleaning Washing or removing dirt stains or writing.

Crease Slight tears where a note has been folded, possibly even a separation of the paper fibers on the line where the crease occurs.

Embossing Indented or raised paper made from printing pressure on the lettering or other parts of the design. Can also be ink above the surface of the note.

Fr. # The most widely used currency numbering system known as the Friedberg Numbering System and developed by Robert Friedberg.

F Fine. A note with more than six folds. Little, if any, crispness will remain.

Gem Gem crisp uncirculated. An almost perfect note. Better than average margins with good centering on both sides. Will have no folds, bends or wrinkles, pinholes or toning.

Margins The paper border from the design of the note to the edge of the note.

MILT# Numbering system for Postage and Fractional Currency developed by Milton R. Friedberg. The only system to number every different note of Postage and Fractional Currency. (Note: The Friedbergs are unrealted.)

Ink Burn A hole in a note caused by an excess of acidic ink.

KL# A numbering system for currency used by Krause Publications, named for Chester L. Krause and Robert F. Lemke.

Pinholes Small, pin-sized holes in a note, caused by staples or from being pinned to a board or other notes.

Proof Notes printed on one side from adopted designs and were not issued for circulation (e.g. Grant/Sherman notes).

Sheet Position Letter

Sheet Position Number

Sheet Position Indicator

On some third issue notes, these indicate the position of the specific note on the sheet. See illustration, page ##.

Sleeper Notes that are underpriced compared to their rarity.

Specimen As used by the Treasury for Fractional Currency, a term meaning an 'example of'.

Toning The aging of paper. Characterized by a light brown or yellowing appearance. Caused by too much exposure to light or sometimes chemicals.

Trimming Cutting paper off a note (mostly wide-margin proofs) to hide or get rid of a fold or some other detect.

VG Very Good. A well-worn note. Will have many folds, most are well soiled. It may also have small tears, pinholes or other signs of circulation.

VF Very Fine. A circulated note that will have four to six folds.

Vignette Portrait or picture. On Fractional Currency, it is on the front of the notes.

Watermark A translucent design or letters pressed into the paper during manufacture, mostly visible when backlit (held up to a light).

XF Extra Fine. A circulated note that will have two or three folds.

Application for Membership to the Fractional Currency Collector's Board

Name: ______________________________

Address: ______________________________

City: ______________________________

State: ______________ Zip: ______________

Work Phone: ______________ Home Phone: ______________

Email Address: ______________________________

Are you: ❑ A Collector ❑ A Dealer ❑ Both

Date Submitted: ______________________________

Membership Recommended by: Rob Kravitz

May we include your address in our membership list? ❑ Yes ❑ No

Please enclose a check for (check one):

$200.00– SPECIAL Lifetime Membership, includes both Simplified and Com-plete versions of Milton Friedberg's *Encyclopedia of United States Postage and Fractional Curren*

$22.00 – to cover new member dues plus a copy of the "Simplified Edition" the *Encyclopedia of United States Fractional and Postage Currency*, by Milton Friedberg.

$30.00– to cover new member dues, the "Simplified Edition" of the Encyclop-dia and the Complete Version of the Encyclopedia.

$15.00 – to cover member's annual dues after the first year of membership, including re-activating membership.

Please forward this application for membership and your dues check (made out to th FCCB) to:

The FCCB

c/o Bill Brandimore

Membership Chariman

1009 Nona

Wausau, Wisconsin 54403